MOTHERS OF NATIONS

ACTIVATING WOMEN FOR GLOBAL IMPACT

Dr. Sharon Predovich

Mothers Of Nations
Copyright © 2014 by Sharon Predovich
ISBN: 978-0-942507-96-6
ISBN (E-book): 978-0-942507-97-3

Unless otherwise noted, all Scripture references are from New King James Version. Copyright © 1982 by Thomas Nelson, Inc. Used by permission. All rights reserved.

Scripture quotations marked "Amp" are taken from the Amplified® Bible, Copyright © 1954, 1958, 1962, 1964, 1965, 1987 by The Lockman Foundation Used by permission. (www.Lockman.org)

Scripture quotations marked "NIV" are from The Holy Bible, New International Version®, NIV® Copyright © 1973, 1978, 1984, 2011 by Biblica, Inc.™ Used by permission. All rights reserved worldwide.

Scripture quotations marked "ASV" are from the American Standard Version, Thomas Nelson and Sons, 1901. Public domain in the United States.

Scripture quotations marked "KJV" are taken from The Holy Bible, King James Version, Cambridge, 1769. Public domain.

Address all personal correspondence to:
Pastor Sharon Predovich
Resurrection Life Church
16397 Glory Lane, Eden Prairie, MN 55344
Phone: 952-934-5433
Website: www.rezlife.org
Website: www.mothersofnations.com
Email: mothersofnations@aol.com

Individuals and church groups may order books from either Sharon Predovich directly or the publisher. Retailers and wholesalers should order from our distributors. Refer to the Deeper Revelation Books website for distribution information, as well as an online catalog of all our books.

Published by:
Deeper Revelation Books
Revealing "the deep things of God" (1 Cor. 2:10)
P.O. Box 4260
Cleveland, TN 37320
Phone: 423-478-2843
Website: www.deeperrevelationbooks.org
Email: info@deeperrevelationbooks.org

Deeper Revelation Books assists Christian authors in publishing and distributing their books. Final responsibility for design, content, permissions, editorial accuracy, and doctrinal views, either expressed or implied, belongs to the author.

*" … I will bless her,
and she shall be a*
Mother of Nations;
*kings of people
shall be of her."*

Genesis 17:16b (KJV)

TABLE OF CONTENTS

"THANK YOU"

I would like to say thank you to my loving husband, companion, and friend Bill who has always encouraged me to follow the Lord. He's been a source of comfort, strength, and encouragement for over forty years now.

I also want to thank my daughter and her family as well as my son and his family. For many, many years they have put up with a traveling mother / grandmother who seems to never run out of people to help, places to go, or churches to encourage. You have been my pride and joy and delight!

A very special thank you goes to my dear administrator Rev. Nola Beintema who has spent countless hours editing, reading, and re-reading this book's content to make sure we have honored the Lord in our words and reports. Nola, you are an incredible gift from God in my life!

There have been multiple women in my life that mothered, mentored, and trained me, and to them I am so grateful. As well there have been special men who imparted leadership skills and insights from their life experiences. I thank them all for their heart and for their personal care. In unique ways they each helped to form and mold me into a Mother of Nations.

Thank you to my church family at Resurrection Life who have faithfully prayed, sown seeds, and believed in their Pastor's call. You are the best people a Pastor could ever ask to shepherd!

There are special people in this world who are "hidden gems" in God's Kingdom and to you I am honored to know. This includes Rev. Chris Harken for faithfully interceding for me for years and years at all hours of the day and night. Thanks also to Mike Shreve who encouraged me to put this message in print.

Finally, I thank the Lord for the special privilege of imparting His love and grace into the lives of the people of this world. As a Mother of Nations, this is an honor and calling that I treasure dearly.

FOREWORD

I deeply appreciate the privilege and honor of writing the Foreword to this marvelous book *Mothers of Nations* for the following four reasons:

First and foremost, Pastor Sharon and her husband, Pastor Bill Predovich, have been dear friends for many years. I have had the privilege of staying in their home and ministering in their church. Theirs is a congregation that flows with the power of God, a great group of believers impacting their city and world in a very relevant way. I have found both Bill and Sharon Predovich to be very gracious, kind, sincere and compassionate servants of God—extremely committed to the advancement of the Kingdom of God. So I know first-hand that this book is not just a clever concept Pastor Sharon hopes to promote in order to have a 'successful book.' It is a reality, a lifestyle that has been effectively lived out and transferred to others.

Second, I love being associated with something that is on the cutting edge, a fresh prophetic word to the Body of Christ. In over 40 years of studying God's Word and reading Christian literature extensively, I cannot recall ever seeing a book on this powerful and motivating subject. Being able to 'put my hand to the plow' of this project, to break new ground for the Body of Christ, has been an exhilarating experience.

Third, I have been personally impacted by a Mother of Nations myself, so I know the power of the message. The late Bertha Madden, founder and pastor of the House of Hope in Tampa, Florida, greatly influenced my life. In the fall of 1970 Bertha read an article about me in the Tampa Tribune newspaper, how I was conducting yoga classes at four universities in the area. About three hundred students were attending my classes and I thought the article would cause that number to grow dramatically. Little did I know that God would use it in a much more significant way.

I was a sincere seeker of truth, but unfortunately, I was embracing and promoting false concepts about the nature of God and the pathway to oneness with God. While other Christians in that city may have felt appalled or concerned, as a Mother of Nations, Bertha Madden took action. She refused to sit back idly and watch New Age concepts invade her community. She launched a bold counter-offensive measure 'in the Spirit,' by the authority God had invested in her. Calling her prayer warriors together, she declared the goal of my conversion as an object of intercession. For the next four weeks, every hour of every day, someone was fasting and praying for my salvation. It was no coincidence that at the end of that prayer vigil, one of the members of their 25-member prayer group just 'happened' to pick me up hitchhiking and lead me to the LORD. So again, I know first-hand the power that a true Mother of Nations can wield.

The final reason I am very excited about this book is the anticipation I feel—the inner 'knowing' that it will stir up many great women of God to do the work they have been called to do. So many have felt intimidated or limited because of their gender and the work of God has suffered greatly as a result. Yet these are considered 'the last days,' a time when both "menservants AND maidservants...will prophesy" (Acts 2:18). Such a spiritual urgency is hovering over this generation! How important this revelation is going to be for many! So to my respected co-laborer in the harvest, Apostle/Pastor Sharon Predovich, I echo gripping words that were uttered to another Mother of Nations many centuries ago,

"Who knows whether you have come to the kingdom for such a time as this?" (Esther 4:14)

Mike Shreve
Founder / Director
Deeper Revelation Books

INTRODUCTION

For many years now I have been active as a woman in ministry, from my first experience as a Sunday School teacher at the age of twelve to my present position as a pastor of a strong and growing church in Eden Prairie, Minnesota, USA. The LORD called me to Him at a very young age. Why I was called so early I am not sure, but I cannot remember a day in my life that God was not in my heart or mind. As a young teenager, I dreamed of being a martyr for Christ. Joan of Arc had made such an impression on my life. The stories of *The Robe* and Dale Evans' book called *Angel Unaware* motivated me to seek the LORD and understand Him more.

At age eleven my father was driving my brothers and me to a hospital in Duluth to visit my mother. Much to our shock, he told us that she was dying of a cancerous brain tumor and had less than two years to live. That day my childhood ended and I became the mother of two younger brothers and a baby sister. Having no one to really help me or talk to me about taking care of a home and kids, the LORD became my confidant and my strength. To this day I find myself always seeking His advice and His ways.

I tell this story to explain that this book called *Mothers of Nations* is birthed out of years of experience in both the natural and spiritual realms. Having learned motherhood from an early age, I cannot say I am an expert on it, but I am a survivor. Sometimes the road of motherhood is difficult and painful. Sometimes it is the most rewarding experience in life.

What is a Mother of Nations and how do you become one? Read on and hopefully as these chapters unfold, you will not only desire to be one, but you will step out and do something to actually become one.

CHAPTER 1

WHAT IS A MOTHER OF NATIONS?

"And I will bless her and also give you a son by her;
then I will bless her, and she shall be a
mother of nations;
kings of peoples shall be from her"
(Genesis 17:15-16)

Mothers represent so many different things to each of us. For some, a mother is the one who gave them birth or the woman who raised them. To others, a mother is the one who taught them, trained them, and drove them to school. For some, a mother is a best friend. I have heard mothers called "the one who gave me hope — the one who gave me strength and kept me going—the one who made our home fun and inviting—the one I could not live without."

Mothers can shape us, mold us, scold us, correct us, love us, support us, and care for us. They often instill beliefs, pray for us, and awaken confidence in us. When we know they are counting on us, it makes us want to succeed all the more. They have a way of making their children feel valued. Most certainly, mothers are unique and special. God knew when He created woman that He had completed creation and made the perfect match for the male—a female.

When we go to the Scriptures and read about the woman, we discover that in the beginning of Genesis, she was given by God to Adam as a wife and soon became a mother. Eve gave birth to two boys called Cain and Abel. Later Adam called her "the mother of all living" (Genesis 3:20). Her life in the Garden of Eden before sin was wonderful. But following

Adam and Eve's disobedience to God, life became painful and childbearing fraught with far more complications. Eve experienced the pain of the birth of a child, the pain of the death of a child, and the pain of the exile of a child. Motherhood was often neither pleasant nor joyful, as life itself under the curse of sin brought fear, agony, depression, and so many other negatives. The begetting, conceiving, and birthing of offspring continued with little change to the spiritual condition of the human race (except for Noah and his family) until the time of Abraham and Sarah, when an important and dramatic shift took place.

This story of Abraham and Sarah is an important one, because in it the term Mother of Nations is first found. As I was reading one of my favorite chapters in the Bible, Genesis 12, the Holy Spirit began to speak to me about "Fathers and Mothers to the Nations." God first led Abram to a new land. He was a "sent one," a man on a mission from God. He willingly left the comforts of home and familiar surroundings because of his faithfulness to God. Abram knew not what would come, but trusted that God had created him with a purpose and He had authored a plan that would unfold far into the future.

Later in Genesis 17:2, Abram obeyed God's command to go to this new land. God spoke to him saying, "… *I will make My covenant between Me and you, and will multiply you exceedingly.*" Abram was overwhelmed by God's presence and fell on his face. God spoke to him again, saying:

> "*As for Me, behold My covenant is with you, and you shall be the **father of many nations**.*
>
> *No longer shall your name be Abram, but your name shall be Abraham, for I have made you a **father of many nations**.*

> *I will make you exceedingly fruitful; and **I will make nations of you**, and kings shall come from you."*
> (Genesis 17:4-6)

God told Abraham his destiny, the purpose for which he was created. Notice that God did not put it in the future tense. He declared it in the past tense, as if it was already an established fact: *"I have made you a **father of many nations.**"* When God ordains something, it will definitely come to pass, so He *"calls those things that do not exist as though they did"* (Romans 4:17). It was a 'done deal' as far as heaven was concerned.

Since we were children, many of us heard and even sang the song "Father Abraham." The words, "Father Abraham had many sons, many sons had Father Abraham. I am one of them, and so are you, so let's just praise the LORD, right arm … " echoed loudly as children swung arms, marched, turned around, sat down, and giggled. We accepted and embraced Abraham as a spiritual Father.

As I meditated on this scripture, I saw that God also spoke to Sarai, calling her simultaneously to be the "Mother of Many Nations." He changed her name to Sarah (which means "princess" or "mother of princes") and told her that kings of people would come from her.

> *Then God said to Abraham, "As for Sarai your wife, you shall not call her name Sarai, but Sarah shall be her name.*
> *And I will bless her and also give you a son by her; then I will bless her, and she shall be a **mother of nations;** kings of peoples shall be from her."* (Genesis 17:15-16)

The Holy Spirit began to reveal to me that we need both Fathers and Mothers of Nations to come forth. The two are

17

essential in birthing and developing the kings and leaders of the nations. It was His plan from the beginning.

God wanted to Father and Mother His children through Abraham and Sarah's seed. They were to work side by side and produce offspring by faith. Their offspring would have great leadership skills and become kings of peoples. Abraham laughed because he could not see what God was saying to him. His wife was old and beyond childbearing years. He could not envision this aged woman producing any sons or daughters. Abraham loved Sarah and he respected her, but could not see kings in their future. But God saw it! He destined them for such a time and such a calling.

When Sarah heard of her future, she laughed because she could not see God producing fruitfulness from barrenness. As a woman, Sarah saw her limitations, age, unworthiness, cultural norms, and lack. But God saw her fruit and His purpose.

The prevailing culture has kept women corporately in a state of barrenness for centuries. Apparently God has allowed this, waiting for the fullness of His time when He would awaken them to a time of fruit-bearing. Some women have broken through the walls of this constraint, but many have struggled just to remain personally nourished and healthy in the Kingdom of God. Rules, cultural restrictions, prejudices, fear, and other obstacles have stood in the way. Women have been wrestling to get pregnant with vision. Both men and women have been unable to see the fullness of God's plan. Both have laughed at God, His promises, and His purpose, just as Abraham and Sarah did.

In the course of religious freedom, many have decided that they, as part of creation, knew more than their Creator. God created man and woman in His own image. One part of Him is not inferior to another. The Holy Spirit and Jesus are not inferior to the Father. They are one, the Trinity—one God, comprised of three distinct manifestations—distinct, but not divided. In a similar way, man and woman were made to be one. They were to rule and reign together, having dominion and multiplying throughout the earth. The Bible clearly says that God gave this calling to both of them, not just Adam:

> *Then God blessed **them**, and God said to **them**, "Be fruitful and multiply; fill the earth and subdue it; have **dominion** over the fish of the sea, over the birds of the air, and over every living thing that moves on the earth."* (Genesis 1:28)

Women have accomplished some great things, but the full fruit of Mothers of Nations is yet to be seen. Part of the problem is that they have not yet been recognized as Mothers of Nations. Typically, we refer to the patriarch Abraham as the "Father of Nations," but this exalted status is rarely shared with the matriarch, Sarah. However, the mandate from God included them both. Unfortunately, this is still a tendency even in the Church, denying women any important or authoritative roles in the work of God. Neither Abraham nor Sarah could have accomplished this vision individually. It took them both and so it is today. The task is too great! It is time for women to rise to leadership, not to overrule men, but to take their position beside them. Through the unity of the two, we shall see great fruit borne, great leaders equipped, and great advance for the Kingdom of God. Even kings and queens will be stirred and emerge, under the anointing, to bring revival to the nations and transformation to the world. It has happened many times before and it can easily happen again.

Fathers and Mothers, it is time to bring forth children, to raise up kings, and to parent the nations! We must stop arguing and debating non-essential issues and get right down to the root of the matter. God wants relationship and dominion. He is God and we are His children. He did not ask for a boy and get a girl. He created us both and gave us a purpose and destiny together. Abraham and Sarah were first introduced to childbearing through divine visitations. However, between the oracles they received from God and the actual event were many, many years of barrenness. Likewise, in the beginning of the Church, on the day of Pentecost, Peter declared that in the New Covenant both "sons and ... daughters will prophesy," but similarly, since then, women in the Body of Christ have experienced many years of barrenness (Acts 2:17). The gifts and talents of women have all too often been suppressed, and consequently, men and women have failed to work together as one. Now that awareness of this issue is coming to the forefront, let's work together to produce fruit and to rejoice in the results of our united efforts.

In the New Testament, Jesus explained in a parable that the Kingdom of heaven is like a mustard seed which a man took and sowed in his field. In the very next parable He depicted a woman hiding leaven in three measures of meal until the whole loaf was leavened (Matthew 13:31-33). In this world, usually it is men who plant seeds to produce crops, which in turn supply grain. Usually it is the women who take that grain, grind it, then mix in the leaven (a fungus), knead the dough and bake it to produce loaves of bread. So both are complementary and equally important in their roles and both are needed - in this natural process and in the spiritual process it represents. Producing 'spiritual bread' (the "bread of life") to feed the starving masses will necessarily involve a joint effort as well.

In like manner, God is looking for Fathers to build nations and develop the Kingdom and He is looking for Mothers to nurture and teach nations so that the Church may be nourished and grow to a greater level of maturity and impact. That is why many men are sensing an unction and need to father and many women are feeling an unction and need to mother. The Church itself has cried out for Mothers and Fathers—how much more does the world need them? We are to lead peoples and nations. We must cry out for the release of women and men to work together to parent the nations. Impregnate us with vision, oh LORD, and give us the ability to birth full term babies. Fathers of Nations, it is time to release the seed of God's Word and plant it into the hearts of Mothers of Nations that they might become spiritually pregnant with destiny and further the Kingdom of God.

May we raise kings in the earth and in heaven!

Female leaders are desperately needed in the world today. Not just in the Church, but everywhere. I am convinced the world would be a better place in which to live had women been allowed to preach. Women can speak to the heart, stir up emotions, set hearts and cities ablaze, and pick out a seducing devil a mile away. Life has become so complicated with all its choices, languages, diversity, and the like, yet out of the midst of it, God is calling women. He is calling women to rise up and lead, women who will mother the little ones in the faith and help train them in the way they should go. He is calling Mothers of Nations who know their LORD and know how to find strength in Him. He is challenging Mothers of Nations to walk in authority, filled with the Spirit and dedicated to the Word. He is awakening Mothers of Nations who have vision enough to set a course that will change their world. These will be women focused enough to stay with the direction God gives and courageous enough to reject what will not work to complete the God-inspired vision.

As I looked into Church history regarding women, I discovered many female pioneers who have paved the way for us.

AMANDA SMITH (1837–1915), according to historical records, was an African-American woman, who was born into slavery and feared white people. But one particular Sunday the Spirit of God led her to attend a white church to hear the message of a certain preacher. During that service the Holy Spirit clearly spoke to her out of Galatians 3:28, *"There is neither Jew nor Greek, slave nor free, male nor female, for you are all one in Christ Jesus."* That one moment with the LORD changed the course of her life radically and thrust her into ministry, both at home and abroad. This Mother of Nations ministered in England, Africa, and India where she particularly had great impact and gained a reputation of being known as "God's image carved in ebony." Eventually she founded the Amanda Smith Orphans' Home for African-American children in a Chicago suburb.[1]

CATHERINE BOOTH, another Mother of Nations, was born in 1829 and lived until 1890. It was not until 1860 that she first started preaching when an overcoming compulsion to rise and speak came upon her in a church meeting. Her sermon was so impressive that her husband William Booth completely changed his opinion of women preachers! Despite gaining a reputation as an outstanding speaker for Christ, public opinion was that a woman's place was in the home and any woman who spoke in public risked grave censure and strict consequences.[2]

In 1865 the Booths started London's East End Christian Mission which later became The Salvation Army. Interestingly, at that time William became known as the General and Catherine was called the *Mother of the Salvation Army*. Catherine took a major role in revival meetings, held her own campaigns, and often preached in the dockland parishes. She helped to extend the message of the Gospel beyond church walls, including the organization of the Food for the Million Shops where the poor could buy soup and dinners for just a sixpence. Along with working with the poor, she also spoke to the wealthy, gaining support for the financially demanding ministry outreaches.[3]

ISABELLA GRAHAM and her married daughter, JOANNA BETHUNE, started the Sunday School movement around 1816. She yearned for revival and collected sermons on this subject and then forwarded them to friends in New York, including her daughter. These women then started praying for revival and eventually in 1816 created the "Female Union for the Promotion of Sabbath Schools in New York City." In a day when women could not vote and were considered 'pushy' for being leaders, they began planting Sunday schools and at the same time empowered women. Working with children was one of few ways ladies could minister in most congregations at that time. Accused of breaking the Sabbath by holding classes on Sunday, these two women held onto the words of the LORD who said, *"Suffer the little children to come unto Me."* (Mark 10:14 KJV)[4]

SALLY PARSONS, though she was young, poor, uneducated, and disowned by her family, insisted that God had called her to work in His harvest fields as a preacher in the late 1790s and early 1800s. Risking rejection she testified of her conversion and in turn the Free Will Baptists praised her as a devout believer who was truly inspired by God. Her ministry was compared to Phoebe, Priscilla, and other women who had worked with Paul in the early Church. Parsons became recognized as a spiritual sister who was "chosen out of the world" to convert sinners.[5] In 1797 enough money was raised to buy a horse, bridle, and saddle for her personal use in ministry so she rode preaching up and down the state of New Hampshire. She remained steadfast in her commitment and radically impacted her generation.[6]

CLARISSA DANFORTH, born in 1792, had a conversion experience in 1809 at seventeen years of age. She became known as "the sensation preacher of the decade," ministering as an itinerant throughout northern New England. As she held revivals and helped start many churches, her ministry easily crossed denominational lines though Danforth was the first woman ordained as a Free Will Baptist minister.[7]

One of my favorite Mother of Nations stories is about MARY FISHER. She immigrated to the American colonies in 1656 from Barbados where Quakers had set up missionary work. She believed God had called her to the Americas to spread her Quaker beliefs.

Upon arrival in Boston, the authorities became hostile due to her 'liberal' Quaker teachings of sexual equality and opposition to slavery. The Puritans thought she was a witch, and at the age of thirty-three they put her in prison for five years. She was given little food and the windows of her cell were boarded shut so she could not communicate with anyone. Hungry and abused, Fisher prayed for deliverance from this horrible ordeal. An innkeeper was able to bribe her jailer to smuggle food into her cell weekly. After five weeks she was sent home to England on the same ship that had brought her to Massachusetts.[8]

Despite all these trials and tribulations in obeying the voice of the LORD, Fisher again believed that she had heard from God, this time sensing the need to go to the Ottoman Empire in 1658. Arriving in Smyrna, she asked the English

Consul how to contact the Turkish Sultan. He told her she was a foolish woman and put her on a ship to Venice. Fisher left that ship at the next port and journeyed all alone until she reached the Turkish headquarters. She traveled 600 miles on foot over land looking for Sultan Mohammed IV and his army of 20,000. She found the Sultan and said to him that she had a message from the "Great God." The Sultan received her as an ambassador, believed her message, and he said everything she spoke was true.[9] This woman as a Mother of Nations felt the call to these people and off she went. Her labor was not in vain.

There are so many more spiritual mothers worth mentioning that have made great impact, some regionally, others globally. We could compile a large list just from the last one hundred years, including powerful women of God like Aimee Semple McPherson, Kathryn Kuhlman, Gwen Shaw, and Ruth Heflin. Most certainly there are thousands of others we may never know about until we arrive in heaven.

Speaking of Gwen Shaw, at one of the very first charismatic meetings I ever attended, she was the guest speaker. She talked about the call of women to go into the nations and preach. At the end of Sister Gwen's message she gave an altar call for women to give their lives to the LORD and to this call, even if it meant prison, famine, or death. I remember wondering if I could respond, as I had two small children at that time. The Holy Spirit gently spoke to me, "My grace is sufficient for thee." Immediately I was up at that altar in the front row of responders, surrendering to my LORD. That decision changed the course of my life to eventually become a Mother of Nations.

Gwen Shaw and all these other women are wonderful examples of Mothers of Nations. Each one was unique and each one was called by God. There are certain attributes they all had in common. These women were courageous, powerful, prayer warriors, risk-takers, pioneers, faith-walkers, visionaries, love-beings, and servants. They were women of wisdom, prophetic, apostolic, of a royal blood line, and knew their God.

Watch for Mothers of Nations to arise in the days ahead! We are about to see many women coming forward with powerful anointings on their lives. What will this kind of woman look like? She will be a female leader prepared by God, who is passionate to bring change in her generation, and who has understanding concerning her times. Her qualities are identifiable, admirable, and transferrable. This hallowed status can be passed from one generation to the next, from one anointed individual to the next.

As we have already established, Eve was called the "Mother of All Living," found in Genesis 3:20. Then many years later Sarah was called the "Mother of Nations." (Genesis 17: 15) But it didn't stop there! As the mantle was passed on, Rebekah was referred to prayerfully by her family members as a "Mother of Thousands of Millions." (Genesis 24:60 KJV)

And there have been thousands more.

Now, in these latter days, we are compassed about with a cloud of witnesses, from both the Old and New Testament eras. We have a grandstand full of true spiritual Mothers, stretching from the beginning of time to the modern age in which we live. Each one exhibited impressive qualities, necessary for this calling, which others sought to emulate. These, and many others like them, have done special things to make God's plan for the earth succeed. They comforted, showed kindness, saved people, reached out beyond their families to help others, brought forth children, weaned them, awakened leadership in their sons and daughters, ministered the Gospel, and followed their God-given calling.

There are certain women described in the New Testament who possessed Mother of Nations attributes. They followed Jesus, anointed Jesus, kept Jesus' sayings in their heart, did what Jesus said, and declared His glory among the people. They fulfilled the calling in their day. But now the nations are crying out again. Humanity is desperate to hear new voices emerge, desperate for new Mothers to arise.

In the succeeding chapters we will examine the qualities found in a true Mother of Nations. I pray you will find them in yourself, and if not, pursue them until you do. Then, may you dare to stir these qualities up in others, that the existence of Mothers of Nations will not only be a thing of the past, but a reality of the future—not only the stuff of history, but the stuff of prophecy unfolding before our very eyes.

MOTHERS OF NATIONS

CHAPTER 2

MOTHERS OF NATIONS ARE COURAGEOUS

"Courage is fear that has said its prayers."[10]
Karl Barth, a Swiss Reformed theologian

Courage is the quality or state of mind or spirit enabling one to face danger or hardship with bravery. Courage, according to Merriam Webster's Collegiate Dictionary, means "mental or moral strength to venture, persevere, and withstand danger, fear or difficulty." A comment often heard is, "Courage is not the absence of fear, but the conquering of fear."[11]

The word courage comes from an original French word *coeur* that means "heart." Women who manifest courage for the work of God are normally those who have a real heart, a true passion to rise above their own feelings of inadequacy and the rejection of others, to seize *"the mark for the prize of the high calling of God in Christ Jesus"* (Philippians 3:14 KJV). Their deep, abiding love for the things of God overrides their fear of people or their fear of failure. How true it is that *"perfect love casts out fear"!* (1 John 4:18)

A courageous woman can meet strain or difficulty head-on without flinching and continue in that stance for long periods of time with fortitude and resolve. This reminds me of the time when God promised to awaken such a mindset in the prophet Ezekiel, saying:

> *"Like adamant stone, harder than flint, I have made your forehead; do not be afraid of them, nor be dismayed at their looks, though they are a rebellious house."* (Ezekiel 3:9)

This metaphor simply meant Ezekiel would be given the strength of mind, the stubborn faith, to unashamedly speak God's Word and not flounder in times of opposition. This is the very scripture God gave me when I started in ministry. I realized then and there that He would give me the courage to do what He was calling me to do.

A courageous Mother of Nations can, as some people say, "hold her own." That means she can keep going when threatened, ridiculed, misunderstood, or condemned. Courageous Mothers of Nations are able to come up to the plate and bat in times of uncertainty and distress. They will put their lives on the line for those in their charge, defending the Church against all enemy intrusion, no matter what cost may be demanded.

I remember that in August of 1998 I had scheduled leaders' conferences in Nairobi, Kenya, and in Kampala, Uganda. One week before our ministry team was to leave the United States for this outreach, we learned that the U.S. Embassy in Nairobi had been bombed, along with a simultaneous embassy attack in Dar es Salaam, Tanzania. Hundreds of people were killed and there were rumors of possible bombings in Uganda as well. This was an international crisis and our ministry itinerary was about to collide with it!

With just days remaining before our departure for Africa, several people called to discourage me from going. But the LORD assured me that our team would be safe. I gave each member of the team the option to stay back, but all the women in this group chose to move forward. The day we walked into the airport baggage claim area in Nairobi, I knew our decision was right. Our national contacts were astounded to see that we had followed through on our original commitment, regardless of the latest circumstances.

The very first place we ministered in Nairobi was only blocks away from the U.S. Embassy that was bombed. I spoke on the topic "God Has Not Given Us a Spirit of Fear." The Kenyans in that meeting said that the LORD had used us to bring a calming assurance to them that God had everything under control. Our tangible presence in their nation gave them hope and assurance that God's people keep working night and day despite obstacles and challenges.

After our ministry in Kenya, we flew to Uganda to hold conferences there as well. Despite the threats of more bombings, we ministered to over 5,000 people, meeting leaders from five different nations. The Ugandans specifically mentioned that they were shocked that women had come to minister, not men! By faith we spoke into the hearts of the people in those meetings that the LORD had plans of a better future for them. I thank God that I have since seen that country grow and develop in significant ways. Truly, the LORD honors the courage of a Mother of Nations in both known and unknown ways.

A prime example of this character trait of courage is the Biblical figure Deborah, a woman who came forward for battle when there was a need for deliverance in Israel. Apparently there was no strong coalition until Deborah, the Mother of Nations, said she would be willing to face the enemy. This daring and determined "daughter of Sarah" understood the social paralysis prevailing in her culture and the need for anointed leadership. She is quoted as saying:

*"Village life ceased, it ceased in Israel, until I, Deborah, arose, arose a **mother in Israel.**"* (Judges 5:7)

Deborah purposed to make a difference, to be a history-maker and a world-changer, and she did, yet not for her own aggrandizement.

Far from being selfishly motivated, she confessed:

"My heart is with the rulers of Israel who offered themselves willingly with the people. Bless the LORD!" (Judges 5:9)

Yes, it was all about blessing God and helping others. It was all about assisting those who needed encouragement and an infusion of strength.

In those days the tribe of Benjamin was fierce in battle and Naphtali's warriors were recognized for their bravery and stamina. Zebulun's troops were known for producing scribes and keepers of the Word. Reubenites and male leaders like Barak were functioning as prophets and judges. They were all gifted. They were all blessed with individual areas of strength, but they needed a leader who could rally them together to pursue a common cause - to win in a larger arena.

Deborah sat between two places to rule. One was called Ramah, meaning "the high place," and the other was called Bethel, meaning "the house of God." Surely "the high place" represents the heavenly realm, called "the high and holy place" in Isaiah 57:15. The "house of God" represents His dwelling on earth, the location where He resides among His people. So a Mother of Nations is one who connects these two worlds: heaven and earth. She sits in intercession between the two. She seeks God enough to be familiar with heavenly things, but she relates to human beings enough to be sensitive to their weaknesses and battles. Such was Deborah, and she shines brightly in Scripture as a Mother of Nations.

Deborah had the consensus of other leaders, but courageous Mothers of Nations are also willing to stand alone, if necessary. In the process of going to battle, they may make others angry. Not everyone likes a woman of courage, but they are desperately needed if we are to experience a true heaven-sent visitation in our society and our world. That is why, especially during times of intercession, we often hear statements like, *"Awake Deborahs, and arise!"* For there are many *"Deborahs"* who are asleep to their spiritual potential, their God-given ordination, even some of you who are reading this book.

History has many stories for us of women who made a decision and not everyone liked it. For example, Golda Meir was the fourth prime minister of Israel, known as the "Iron Lady" of Israeli politics. When confronted with the gathering of the Syrian army on the Golan Heights, she at first considered a preemptive attack. However, she also realized that if Israel was perceived as the aggressor, the support of the United States would be impossible to win. So against the advice of one of her chief advisors, she courageously waited until Egypt and Syria launched that offensive now known as the Yom Kippur War (October 6-25, 1973).

Both the United States and Russia stepped in on either side of the battle lines, almost resulting in a global clash of the two super-powers. But Israel's alliance with the United States proved to be the stronger one. This example shows clearly that courage at times can be evidenced more in wisely waiting than rashly running into a conflict. Fools are often impetuous. On the contrary, men and women of courage tend to intelligently assess all their options and then proceed with the decision which is imbued with the most wisdom, regardless of its popularity.

Mothers of Nations operating in courage are not afraid of a challenge, especially if it is related to a cause. Esther is a prime example of this attribute. Being the Queen of Persia, she was a Mother to that empire, as well as a Mother to the Jews. She knew that a mother has to protect her children, and Esther proceeded to do that very thing. Her own life was at risk, but the lives of countless thousands were more important to her than her own. In chapters four through seven of the book of Esther, we read where she devised a plan, one that outwitted the deceitful strategies of wicked Haman and took him completely by surprise. Mothers of Nations are like that. They are intuitive concerning enemy plots and plans, and they are not inhibited about using their intuition to launch a counter-attack for the sake of God's Kingdom.

Not long ago a minister friend, who is also one of my daughters in the Kingdom, shared with me her journey on an outrigger boat to a remote island in the Philippines. When she and the ministry team arrived at the island, they realized that they were on an island where extremely vicious hired murderers lived. Unknown to my friend, people had named that location "Murderers' Island"

Gospel meetings had already been arranged and my friend had no other choice but to move forward with the plans despite these new challenges. Fearful and nervous, she preached and taught the Good News, knowing that she could be killed at any time. But to God be the glory! Men and women came to Christ and lives were miraculously changed. She said it took the supernatural courage given to her by the Holy Spirit to even open her mouth to preach. But with that courage, many lives were changed for eternity.

As we travel on mission trips and bring the Gospel of Jesus Christ to many remote areas around the world, we realize that it is not just individuals, but nations we are saving and bringing to the knowledge of Christ. Whether we face an angry king, a furious cult, or a raving, religious lunatic, we walk in courage. Mothers of Nations are not thinking about themselves, but are meditating, seeking, and asking God what they can do to further His Kingdom. God always has a strategy that will work, and Mothers of Nations wait on Him until He leads them in "a plain path" (Psalm 27:11).

I have experienced being led on a "plain path" many times while ministering in the nations. Once in India the Holy Spirit started to lead me up a path (a literal path!) to a village. Having no idea where I was going, I just followed the prompting of the Holy Spirit. He sovereignly led me to a house where I knocked on the door and the people there invited me and our interpreter inside. Trusting the LORD for the right words to say, I shared the Gospel with the whole household of six members ... and they all received Jesus Christ as Savior. We left that house praising God for leading us on "a plain path" that day!

The courage of Mothers of Nations comes from knowing that the LORD is their helper. Hebrews 13:6 (Amp) tells us:

> *So we take comfort and are encouraged and confidently say, The LORD is my helper. I will not be seized with alarm. (I will not fear or dread or be terrified). What can man do to me?*

When David the shepherd boy went to battle against Goliath, he was not the biggest, the strongest, or the most experienced, but he was the most courageous. His courage came from something invisible, deep inside of him. He knew His LORD as a deliverer and he wanted everyone to know and see God as faithful and true. David's courage astounded his family, even to the point of making them angry. However, it aroused the same courage in all the onlookers. Mothers of Nations, operating in courage based in Christ and not in themselves, are not afraid of an opportunity to win a battle, nor are they afraid to put their lives on the line. Their courage, in like manner, has an awakening effect on others.

CHAPTER 3

MOTHERS OF NATIONS ARE FAITH-WALKERS

"Faith sees the invisible, believes the incredible, and receives the impossible."[12]
Corrie Ten Boom, author of *The Hiding Place*

Faith was given to us when we came to the LORD, but faith is also increased in us as we hear the Word of God and press forward in Him.

For whatever is born of God overcomes the world, and this is the victory that overcomes the world, even our faith. (1 John 5:4)

We walk by faith, not by sight. We are confident and make it our aim to be well pleasing to Him. Bold faith pleases God, and Mothers of Nations are definitely God-pleasers. They know how to go after what they need. A prime example of a woman operating in faith is found in the book of Mark, chapter five. The woman with the issue of blood pressed through the crowd and touched Jesus, seeking for her healing. By faith Mothers of Nations will press into prayer for others. They will cry out to God for healing, deliverance, souls, or whatever the Master has put on their heart to do.

Mothers of Nations are faith-walkers and faith-talkers. They put their focus and their foundation on the Word of God. Their faith grows as they put it into effect. Faith says, "I'm created by God. I'm a dominion-taker, multiplying in the blessings of God." Walking implies progress, taking steps toward a goal, so walking in faith implies growing in faith, progressing, and moving toward your destiny.

Faith opens prison doors, shuts the mouths of lions, keeps us in divine health, and assures us that God directs our path. Every Mother of Nations has been given a certain predestined degree of faith sufficient to fulfill her calling. It's a gift from God. Romans 12:3 reminds us:

> *"For I say, through the grace given to me, to everyone who is among you, not to think of himself more highly than he ought to think, but to think soberly, as God has dealt to each one a measure of faith."*

A Mother of Nations has faith in many areas such as healing, finance, and deliverance. Sometimes she may have stronger faith in one area than in another. Her faith starts out at the level of a child, but grows to maturity through experience, the Word, and obedience to the Holy Spirit.

I have seen and heard of Mothers of Nations with "great faith" or what some Bible versions call "rare faith." "Strong faith" is applied to women who do not waver in unbelief (Romans 4:20). Mothers of Nations can operate on many different levels of faith, ranging from "little," to "weak," to "strong," to "full," to "rich." Here are the Scriptures that identify those categories:

> *But when he [Peter] saw that the wind was boisterous, he was afraid; and beginning to sink he cried out, saying, "LORD, save me!"*
> *And immediately Jesus stretched out His hand and caught him, and said to him, "O you of little faith, why did you doubt?"* (Matthew 14:30-31)

> *And not being weak in faith, he [Abraham] did not consider his own body, already dead (since he was about a hundred years old), and the deadness of Sarah's womb.* (Romans 4:19)

He [Abraham] did not waver at the promise of God through unbelief, but was strong in faith, giving glory to God .... (Romans 4:20)

Now in those days, when the number of the disciples was multiplying, there arose a complaint against the Hebrews by the Hellenists, because their widows were neglected in the daily distribution.

Then the twelve summoned the multitude of the disciples and said, "It is not desirable that we should leave the Word of God and serve tables.

Therefore, brethren, seek out from among you seven men of good reputation, whom we may appoint over this business;

But we will give ourselves continually to prayer and to the ministry of the Word."

And the saying pleased the whole multitude. And they chose Stephen, a man full of faith and the Holy Spirit. (Acts 6:1-5)

Listen, my beloved brethren: has God not chosen the poor of this world to be rich in faith and heirs of the kingdom which He promised to those who love Him?" (James 2:5)

Our goal should be that after years of stepping out in faith, each one of us will become a Mother of mature faith (James 1:2-4), world-overcoming faith (1 John 5:4), and exceeding growing faith (2 Thessalonians 1:3).

Consider it pure joy, my brothers, whenever you face trials of many kinds,

Because you know that the testing of your faith develops perseverance.

Perseverance must finish its work so that you may be mature and complete, not lacking anything. (James 1:2-4 NIV)

For whatever is born of God overcomes the world. And this is the victory that has overcome the world—our faith. (1 John 5:4)

We are bound to thank God always for you, brethren, as it is fitting, because your faith grows exceedingly, and the love of every one of you all abounds toward each other. (2 Thessalonians 1:3)

Hebrews 11 identifies various Fathers and Mothers of Nations who utilized the power of faith and did not perish with others. They subdued kingdoms, worked righteousness, obtained promises, quenched the violence of fire, escaped the edge of the sword, and became valiant in battle. Some even received their dead raised to life again.

Mothers of Nations live by faith. They know how to rejoice in the midst of suffering, endure ill treatment, and keep going. Faith is walked out, worked out, lived out, fought out, and sought out. Faith operating in love cannot be stopped.

CHAPTER 4

MOTHERS OF NATIONS ARE VISIONARIES

"Vision is looking at life through
the lens of God's eye."[14]
Chuck Swindoll, pastor and Christian author

Vision is something that God places in a Mother of Nations to change people, nations, and the world. She sees herself as having a divine purpose on earth and sees that God has a specific plan for her to accomplish that purpose. The Bible tells us about many people to whom God gave vision. For instance, God appeared to Noah and commanded him to build an ark. He gave Noah very detailed instructions on how to build it. Another example is Abraham who was told that he would have as many descendants as the stars of heaven. God imparted to him a vision of many descendants, a Promised Land, a great name, blessings, and divine protection for all nations that blessed Abraham and his offspring.

Gideon was given a vision of victory over the Midianites, Joshua of crossing the Jordan and entering the Promised Land, and John the Baptist of a new era. No matter who God gave the vision to, He required obedience to carry out the plan. He chose people He knew would obey Him and stay faithful to the vision. God may give a vision for a nation or a people group to a Mother of Nations. The vision may come to her in her spirit, in her soul, through a rhema word, in a dream, by someone else, or by some unusual circumstance. No matter how it comes, the woman called to the nations will have an all-consuming desire to fulfill that vision.

Vision is rarely an instant thing. It usually takes time and resources to fulfill a vision. Opposition comes to try and steal, detour, or stop the vision, but God keeps the Mother of Nations pressing forward. Her heart is fixed, her mind is focused, and her faith is anchored in Him alone.

Vision is also for an appointed time so the Mother of Nations cannot give up. Discouragement may try to stop her, but through His strength, she continues on. God's eternal, heavenly purposes are being unveiled today. He is releasing women all over the world and instilling vision into them. They are being divinely called and divinely empowered.

One of the most outstanding things happening today is the calling of women to unite in order to more effectively fulfill their God-given destiny and vision. David's mighty men came together to help him complete his destiny (1 Chronicles 11-14). They fellowshipped with him, suffered with him, and even risked their lives to support him. Equipped and able, they shared their skills, weapons, and heart. They were known for their courage and leadership abilities.

God is raising up female leaders today to network with other female leaders. They are joining hands to help build the Kingdom of God. Like David's mighty men, they are willing to share in the pain, as well as in the glory. They are developing their skills and their education. Many are leading large ministries, churches, and organizations for the Kingdom work. These women are interested in relationships with God and His chosen leaders. They see by revelation that the destiny of the church lies in networking with one another. They understand that we are living in prophetic times and are aware of the problems we face, as well as the solutions.

Recognizing this need for women to network and help one another, I started W.I.M.N. in the late 1990's. The vision of Women's International Ministers' Network (W.I.M.N.) is to establish, encourage, and equip women for excellence in ministry. I found that there is such a precious anointing when called women, especially Mothers of Nations, gather together in friendship and respect to support one another with their spiritual giftings, goals, vision, and prayers.

What woman in God's service doesn't need encouragement from time to time to continue in her ministry's vision? Ruth and Naomi were two unique women with diverse backgrounds, different ages, and distinct family histories. Yet these two ladies developed a lasting friendship that carried them through many trials and triumphs. Each had a season of ministering to the other. My prayer has always been that W.I.M.N. would knit Mothers of Nations together in love and create opportunities for us to help other women in ministry throughout the world.

Mothers of Nations have never really asked to be alone in the field. Most of them ask for helpmates and team workers. Deborah, the female judge in ancient Israel, knew she needed the help of Barak (a man) and Jael (another woman). She was willing to do her part to complete the vision and allowed others to fulfill the roles that God skilled and prepared them to perform.

David's mighty men stayed in their position and rank. Their power together would have been nullified if they had not known how to stay in rank. God desires that we as Mothers of Nations submit to the rank He puts us in. Sometimes we lead and sometimes we follow. Sometimes we team up and sometimes we go alone. No matter where God places us in battle, it is important that we stay within His divine alignment.

I have read and heard multiple stories of women who have

traveled to foreign countries alone to fulfill a dream God gave them. Some have given up everything to fulfill their calling. In my case, appropriately, God launched me into the life of a visionary through the ministry of a woman preacher.

Many of us can look back and remember someone who put vision into our lives or who challenged us to discover who we are in Christ. For me my first experience with a visionary was through a woman revivalist from Orlando, Florida, named Colleen Steinke. She came to my home state to preach at a Full Gospel Businessmen's meeting. Having never seen any minister pray for the sick before, I was amazed when I saw legs and arms grow out to normal lengths. When this minister prayed for back pain in some of the attendees, they were healed!

Following the meeting that night I spent time visiting with Colleen and her husband. I realized I had taught her daughter years before in an elementary school in St. Paul, Minnesota. Through this common bond we became good friends and she started mentoring me in ministry.

As a woman of vision, a revivalist, and a prophet to the nations, Colleen placed many visions into my heart and life. She encouraged me to start a weekly prayer meeting, a ministry to women, and eventually a church. When I had moments of confusion or uncertainty as to what to do in ministry, I would call her for insight and wisdom.

My first time to visit her in Florida my life was completely changed as she instilled such faith in me through her stories of revival. One Tuesday afternoon in the weekly prayer meeting of Colleen's ministry I got so touched by God and His presence that if I could have gone to heaven that day I would have done so! Another day we went into deep prayer and I realized that God was instilling vision for ministry into my heart. In a vision I saw white letters written on a wall that said, "Start a church." And from that direction my husband and I did start a church about two months later on January 7, 1990 – Resurrection Life Church and World Ministry Center.

One of my first mission trips was with this Mother of Nations as well. We traveled to the Philippines and it was on that trip that I realized I had found my niche in life. It was a call to the nations.

As a visionary Colleen also taught me to worship the Lord with all my heart, to pray for God to move supernaturally in the lives of people, and to expect miracles. She was a tremendous Mother in the faith and a gift to me as a young woman learning to walk in ministry and vision.

CHAPTER 5

MOTHERS OF NATIONS
ARE PIONEERS

*"Always use the word impossible
with the greatest of caution."*[15]
Wernher Von Braun,
German engineer involved in space exploration

Pioneers start new things. They are the earliest to settle a place or the ones who pave the way for others. There are women in Church history that paved the way for us today.

In the 1800s Phoebe Palmer introduced the altar ministry. More recently, Gwen Shaw introduced the term "End-time Handmaidens" and "Servants of the LORD" to the Church world and the secular world as well. Sister Gwen was a pioneer of recruiting prayer warriors and bringing the ministry of the Word to thousands throughout the world. Another woman, Fuschia Pickett, was used by God to pioneer the area of women in ministry, introducing fresh teaching on the Holy Spirit. She was a mentor to many men and women serving in the Kingdom.

Pioneers have a trailblazing spirit in them. They go before others, blazing a trail the rest can follow. Some call them "torchbearers" or "scouts." In the early days of America, we had pioneers who went west in wagon trains looking for gold. The wagon train was comprised of the trail boss who gave the orders, the scout who checked out the territory, cooks who kept the team fed and healthy, hired hands who worked, and travelers who provided help and funds to get to their destinations.

Each person was needed and each one had a specific job that had to be done well in order to make the trip successful. Along the trail they often encountered bad weather, deserts, wild animals, hostile people, mountains, snakes, and various other challenges. The trail boss kept the people united and rallied them together to fight if an enemy attacked. Regardless of the role each person played, when things got tough, they all had to support one another.

Pioneers who are called to be Mothers of Nations are motivated also by a final goal. Paul said in 2 Corinthians 4:18 (KJV), *"While we look not at the things which are seen, but at the things which are not seen, for the things which are seen are temporal, but the things which are not seen are eternal."* Mothers of Nations see the destiny of the Church and they reach for that final goal.

Pioneers are adaptable. Mothers of Nations can continue to press on no matter what difficult conditions they encounter. They could be troubled on every side, yet they will not become distressed, perplexed, nor cast down (2 Corinthians 4:8). Steadfast and responsible, Mothers of Nations know that in the process of pioneering, their labor is not in vain.

They are willing and ready to forgive, not allowing offenses to take over due to the trials and tests they face. They have a mind to work and study to show themselves approved so they can rightly divide the Word of truth (2 Timothy 2:15). Recognizing the importance of staying in rank as a risk-taker, they remain stable and steady in their position.

No pioneer would reach her destination unless she was as bold as a lion. The boldness of an adventurer is visible to all. The Mother of Nations is as meek as a lamb until the voice of the lion is needed. Lions know what territory is theirs and they only need to roar to let the whole area know that they are protecting their domain.

Mothers of Nations operating in their pioneering spirit are manifesting that fearless and ferocious "lion" kind of anointing. They are visionaries who joyfully tackle great challenges. They are innovators, forerunners, explorers, and developers. They forge ahead of the pack—those who rarely, if ever, challenge the status quo. With problem-solving skills, focused vision, and purpose, they make things happen. They know when to push forward blazing the trail and when to stop at the oasis to rest.

CHAPTER 6

MOTHERS OF NATIONS
ARE RISK-TAKERS

"The sea is a dangerous place and its storms terrible,
but these obstacles have never been
sufficient reason to remain ashore."[15]
Ferdinand Magellan, explorer

Hollywood has its stars that come and go. Even Christian television has its personalities that are pushed to the forefront, building their ministries through the airwaves. The Bible also has its "stars," the outstanding characters that shine in an extraordinary way. They are not just more talented or charismatic than others, but rather the hand of God is very evidently upon their lives. Esther was definitely a "star" in the Old Testament. In fact her name in Persian actually means "star." Her story is one of a Mother of Nations, for Esther became the queen of the Persian Empire.

The story of Esther begins just before that great empire fell to Alexander the Great in 331 B.C. Esther and her uncle Mordecai lived in Susa, a political, cultural, and religious city in Persia. It was the capital city of a vast network of conquered countries, stretching across three continents: Asia, Europe, and Africa.

The first queen of the empire was named Vashti. For one hundred and eighty days the king displayed to all his officials and allies the splendor of his kingdom. The king ended his big celebration with a seven-day banquet. On the final day of the banquet, the king issued an order for the queen to come and display her beauty. In those days one could never enter the king's presence without an invitation or a summons.

Vashti was supposedly hosting her own feast for the women at the palace and refused to come. Some historians think she may have been pregnant and did not want to be paraded in front of men in that condition.

Needless to say, the king was humiliated, embarrassed, angry, and frustrated in front of his officials. She made him look weak and powerless. After discussing the situation with his leaders, the king decided she must be banished and replaced with a new queen. Through an amazing and miraculous series of events, Vashti was replaced with an orphan girl called Esther. Esther rose to the occasion and became a queen with a heart to serve others but she was challenged from the very beginning of her reign.

Why is Esther considered a Mother of Nations? Why was she a risk-taker and what are risk-takers like?

Esther, as a Mother of Nations, was thrust into the midst of a national crisis. She was urged by her uncle Mordecai to intervene and use her influential position of authority to stop the decree of the enemy to kill all the Jews. Her life unfolded in a very unexpected way. She started out as just an ordinary girl living an ordinary life when destiny suddenly stepped in and everything changed.

Esther became a woman who lived a life she never could have imagined. Mothers of Nations often end up in situations and even countries where they never expected to be. They do things they have had no previous training to do. Their lives become fertile ground in which the unexpected can grow.

Esther also took risks as a Mother of Nations. Her first step was entering a beauty contest. No woman becomes a heroine without a contest to win. Her whole position in society changed the day she was recognized publicly. Heroes and heroines not only enter contests, but they go through whatever preparation is needed. As a risk-taking woman, Esther allowed people to shape her, mold her, perfume her, and develop her for leadership. She became a woman who walked in favor with God and other people. The beauty contest providentially resulted with her being crowned as queen.

As a Mother of Nations, Esther was a woman of favor at all times and in many situations. She often rose up to assume her rightful leadership role. There are some things risk-takers just know. They know how to keep quiet if it is unnecessary for everyone else to know. They know there is a timing for everything when one lives on the edge. Esther was a Mother of Nations who did not remain in the background. She got involved in society, asked questions, and brilliantly dealt with the enemies of the court. As a risk-taker, Esther was called upon to put her life on the line for God's people. She did this with extraordinary courage and grace.

Mothers of Nations often encounter challenges and perils. Sometimes the "risk" might be to go where no one else will go. More than once the LORD has asked us to go to a country where a bomb had recently exploded or a terrorist group had just attacked. I know of Mothers of Nations who have been in the middle of earthquakes or left towns just before the police came to arrest them. These women are risk-takers for the Kingdom of God. They expect the unexpected. They are prepared to meet the challenges, and they shine like stars in the midst of darkness.

I remember one of our mission trip outreaches to the Philippines in particular where I was challenged to be a risk-taker. We had finished meetings in Lucena City and were asked to travel on to Naga City with that same ministry to hold a large conference. Because it was the Easter holiday season, there were no available flights where all of our team could travel together. The only way to get to our destination was by bus through the mountains and this particular highway was known for many attacks by bandits on passersby.

Honestly, the trip to Naga City was dangerous and we knew that. But the night before we were to depart, we prayed and made a final decision. If the Gospel wasn't worth dying for, why preach it? Anything worth living for should also be worth dying for, we concluded.

At the bus station the next morning we tried to get seats on the first vehicle out, but there were not enough spaces for all of us to travel together for safety reasons. We decided to wait until the next bus departed, but the same thing happened again. Finally we were able to get all our seats on the very last bus of the day that left in the late evening.

Aware of the reports of rebels stopping busses on this route, we kept alert and prayed to ourselves as we traveled. About three hours into the trip we realized that we were in a mountainous area. The roads were very winding and driving was much slower. Suddenly we saw a group of rebels standing on the hill next to the road with guns and large sticks in their hands. Their faces were partially covered and they had rags twisted around the tops of their heads as hats. We quickly shut the curtains on our windows and peeked through the cracks to see what might happen next. Amazingly, no one on that hillside moved! It seemed as though the rebels never saw us as we passed by … to our great delight and relief. When we arrived in the bus station at Naga City we were told that the two busses leaving before us had been stopped, burned, and hostages taken.

Without a doubt the LORD and His angels had protected us, even by having us travel on the last bus of the day out of Lucena City. We realized our decision to follow God was a risk, but also a form of commitment to serving Him through trial, tribulation, or peril. Happy to be safe, we were also happy we had chosen to love the LORD with all our heart … even if it meant loss of life.

Interestingly, a few days into our ministry there in Naga City, our team decided to go out for pizza. As we walked to a restaurant just a block down from our hotel, we saw some big military vehicles coming up the street. Thinking it was the Philippine army coming into town, we continued on to get our food. After dinner we walked back to our hotel and there in the lobby was a table full of uniformed men eating and drinking. Suddenly the man at the head of the table started shouting at me in a tone that I knew was not good. Not realizing who these men were yet, we decided to hurry up to our rooms and pray, just in case these were rebels from the mountains. As I was praying, the LORD gave me Proverbs 3:21-26:

> *My son, let them not depart from your eyes—keep sound wisdom and discretion;*
> *So they will be life to your soul and grace to your neck.*
> *Then you will walk safely in your way, and your foot will not stumble.*
> *When you lie down, you will not be afraid; yes, you will lie down and your sleep will be sweet.*
> *Do not be afraid of sudden terror, nor of trouble from the wicked when it comes;*
> *For the LORD will be your confidence, and will keep your foot from being caught.*

We were safe! The Word of the LORD brought us incredible peace that night as we went to bed. And in the next couple days as we finished our ministry assignment there in Naga

City, I found out that the angry man who yelled at me in the lobby was the leader of the rebels in that mountain region. God protected us!

Often Mothers of Nations take risks not realizing how much of an influence these actions can have on an area or even on a nation. In 2005 one of our mission teams traveled on an outreach to northern Uganda to a city called Gulu. War had impacted that region and the "LORD's Liberation Army" under a leader named Joseph Kony had terrorized the villages all over the north of that nation. Southern Ugandans refused to travel to the north unless absolutely necessary. Many were afraid to journey on the roads as rebel troops would set up roadblocks and confiscate vehicles, take possessions, and terrorize. In some cases parents were killed and their children kidnapped to serve in Kony's army.

The Holy Spirit had spoken to me to go to Gulu and to hold an evangelistic crusade at one of the IDP (International Displaced People) camps. He had also confirmed this outreach effort through my son-in-law and another pastor from Kampala, Uganda. When we arrived at the airport in Uganda my team was met with two military escort vehicles. We had armed soldiers on a truck in front of our van and also following us. They escorted us all the way to Gulu, about a five hour drive from the capital city of Kampala. I was well aware of the emotions and thoughts of a "risk-taker" as we drove into new territory to take the land for the Kingdom of God.

The evangelistic crusades in Gulu were extremely fruitful with over 1,000 people getting saved. Five hundred were water baptized, a new church was started, a boxing gym ministry was birthed, pigs and goats were given to start businesses in the area, and food was distributed to hundreds of families. In just a few days of ministry, a whole city was brought hope. Was the risk worth it? Yes, yes, a thousand times, YES!

I found out later that our ministry trip to Gulu sparked a fire in other ministries and pastors from Kampala (southern Uganda) to go to that region and minister as well. They started holding clothing drives, Gospel meetings, and planting new churches. The fear of going into that territory was broken by one person's willingness to take a risk and obey the assignment of the LORD. That risk led to untold blessing for so many people!

It is true that Mothers of Nations are often used to bring forth significant changes in the world. Had Esther not been willing to jeopardize her own life, multitudes of Jews would have been mercilessly slaughtered. Instead, she became a key to their survival and an integral part of their national history. She passed from obscurity to worldwide fame and acclaim, but only because she simply chose to do the right thing at the right time, regardless of the personal danger. May we dare follow in her footsteps!

CHAPTER 7

MOTHERS OF NATIONS ARE INTIMATE WITH GOD

"Never be afraid to trust an unknown future to a known God."[16]
Corrie Ten Boom, author of *The Hiding Place*

Daniel 11:32 foretells that in the last days, *"The people who know their God shall be strong and carry out great exploits."* Paul pleads in Philippians 3:10 (KJV), *"That I may know Him and the power of His resurrection .... "*

Mothers of Nations are women who have come to know their God. They know His character and His ways. When you are married to someone you get to know them so well that you can sense what that person will or will not do in any given situation.

With God, you come to know His nature and His ways as you serve Him and abide in His Word. The more time spent in His presence, the more a Mother of Nations learns to hear His voice and recognize His words.

She also learns to see His method of operation and yields to it. As a developing Mother of Nations, I came to realize that not only must I know Him, but I must also know myself. My weaknesses needed to be yielded to Him that He might become my strength. My strengths needed to be yielded to Him that I might walk in His ways and not my own.

When a Mother of Nations knows her LORD, she realizes He always wants the best for her. Learning to flow with Him and not against Him, she becomes clay in the Potter's hand.

Mothers of Nations know they are accepted in the

beloved, secure in Him, and significant. They are aware of His divine protection and comfort. David instructed his heir-apparent with these words:

"As for you, my son Solomon, know the God of your father, and serve Him with a loyal heart and with a willing mind; for the LORD searches all hearts and understands all the intent of the thoughts. If you seek Him, He will be found by you .... " (1 Chronicles 28:9)

And so it is for God's leaders in this present age. How can a Mother of Nations know God better? First, she can take time to search the Scriptures. Psalm 119:15-16 says:

I will meditate on Your precepts, and contemplate Your ways. I will delight myself in Your statutes; I will not forget Your Word.

Secondly, she can be willing to step out of her comfort zone and do the things He asks. Mary and Martha both loved God and both wanted to know Him. Mary wanted to know Him by sitting at His feet, listening and learning. Martha wanted to know Him by serving Him. Both were good, but Jesus revealed to Martha that taking time to sit at His feet should come first, and then the serving will automatically follow. We cannot effectively serve without knowing the Master's voice and His ways.

God promises in His Word that knowledge is given to those who diligently seek Him.

My son, if you receive my words, and treasure my commands within you,
So that you incline your ear to wisdom, and apply your heart to understanding;
Yes, if you cry out for discernment, and lift up your voice for understanding,

*If you seek her as silver, and search for her as for
hidden treasures;*
Then you will understand the fear of the LORD, *and
find the knowledge of God.*
For the LORD *gives wisdom; from His mouth come
knowledge and understanding.* (Proverbs 2:1-6)

Mothers of Nations, in their desire to know God, may learn
about many things. I have learned over the years to trust God.
When I read of Bible characters God called to do impossible
tasks, I noticed there was always a time in their lives when it
was necessary for them to simply surrender and trust.

Samson knew God as his source of strength and power.
He also knew God as the faithful One who restores the
repentant and renews their gifts. David also knew God as
the ruler of everything, the One on whom he meditated and
by whom the universe was brought forth in splendor. David
knew God as the One who delivered him, anointed him, and
transformed him from an unknown shepherd boy into a
world-acclaimed king.

Solomon knew God as the One his father followed and
relied upon. He also knew that to be an effective king, he
would need a similar relationship with the Almighty. Later,
he knew Him as the One who could impart supernatural
wisdom. Joshua knew God as the One who possesses the
gates of the enemy, the One who clears the way for His
own to walk into the Promised Land. Gideon learned that
knowing God meant impossible battles could be won and
that one did not have to be from a great family or have a
great name to be successful.

After the pattern of all these great Bible personalities,
Mothers of Nations who know their God will also do great
exploits. This happens, not just from knowing Him, but

from realizing the spiritual identity that we all share in Him and the abilities we possess through Him.

There is one mystery of the faith I have discovered that never ceases to fill my heart with awe. God delights to use ordinary people to do extraordinary things so He can receive all the glory!

CHAPTER 8

MOTHERS OF NATIONS
ARE SERVANTS

*"The service we render to others is the rent we pay
for our room on this earth."*[17]
Wilfred T. Grenfell,
medical missionary to Newfoundland

Mothers of Nations are called to serve. They don't waste their time quarrelling over who is the greatest or the least. They have already passed the essential test of leadership and no longer desire recognition, ranks, or position. They have defeated ambition and pride and are moving on to more important matters.

Servanthood is learning to contribute to the welfare of others. Servants obey their masters and are loyal to them. They do not dwell on their own needs, but rather, focus on God's requests or other people's needs. Mothers of Nations have learned to have a servant's heart through developing their relationship with the LORD. The more His nature has grown in them, the more they desire to serve.

Over the years I have seen many female leaders come and go. The ones who have lasted are those who display a servant's heart. They have been very willing to do the little things as well as the big things. Some have never received much recognition for service, yet they continue to serve. They have hearts that truly treat all people as equals. They do not cater to the rich, neither are the poor neglected by them. They serve according to the call of the LORD and the need of the moment. These servants will fill in wherever and whenever they are needed.

If you desire to be used as a Mother of Nations, you cannot tell God who is important, who you want to help, and where you want to be noticed. True service is a lifestyle. You find yourself serving without even thinking about it.

"Attitude determines altitude." This old saying is very true. If you desire to be an influence in the nations, it starts with an attitude of humility. Jesus said, *"He that is greatest among you shall be your servant"* (Matthew 23:11 KJV). The disciples understood what He meant. They had been arguing over recognition, position, and power. So Jesus informed them that servants have no rights of their own. Jesus even washed their feet to further demonstrate the attitude they needed.

I have discovered that sometimes in the process of serving God's people we have moments where the LORD touches us in a very special way. In reference to this very topic of feet washing, I so clearly remember an incident while ministering at a Pastors' Conference in India when we decided to hold a foot washing ceremony with 300 pastors. We thought it was a "God idea" and set out to get all the supplies needed to thus serve and bless these dear Indian pastors.

I must admit that in my mind I never thought through the whole process culturally so I was not prepared for the effects of that activity. I was just thinking it would be a time of loving and serving God's people in a Biblical way. However, when it came time to individually wash the feet of 300 pastors, I suddenly realized the 'shape' we ministers were in! Our Indian host had broken ribs and could hardly bend over. I was dealing with a bad knee joint and couldn't kneel. The other minister who was traveling with me was struggling with back pain that day. There we were – three misfit musketeers trying to humbly wash feet while each of us was in pain. Thank God for His grace as we were able to minister to each and every pastor that day!

And might I also mention that to my cultural amazement some of the pastors would not come up for us to wash their feet because they thought we were "too holy." I was shocked at their responses and more aware than ever how the disciples must have felt when Jesus washed their feet. Those disciples were really able to understand the heart of the servant by watching Jesus, who gave Himself in service to us all.

Jesus had no problem being a servant because He knew where He came from. He was from royal blood, a descendant from another kingdom with a royal inheritance. He knew His purpose on earth was to reveal His Father's love. He did not have to prove anything to anybody. When He took the position of a slave, He had nothing to lose. People could not sway Him and the devil could not entrap Him. There was no position, wealth, or promise of power, recognition, or honor that could turn His heart from the Father's will.

When a Mother of Nations settles in her heart that she is to take the position of a slave-servant, no demonic force can steal her heart. She no longer needs to prove herself, impress people, or strive to gain attention. She does not care what critics say. She cares more about pleasing her Master. She knows she is from royal blood, her final destination has streets of gold, her life is not her own, and nothing her Lord asks her to do is beneath her. I believe that the Mother of Nation's motto should be, "No greater love has a woman than that she lay down her life for her friends."

How do you recognize a person of such spiritual stature? Dwight Moody said it well:

> *"The measure of a man is not the number of his servants, but the number of people whom he serves."*

CHAPTER 9

MOTHERS OF NATIONS
ARE WISE

"Wisdom is seeing things from God's perspective."[18]
Bill Gothard, Bible teacher and author

There are many ways to look at the word wise. It can be defined as prudent, tactful, sensible, or discreet. Some falsely see being wise as being shrewd, cunning, crafty, or sly. I have also heard it described as educated, enlightened, or smart. For me, using this term for a Mother of Nations means that she is practical, careful, poised, stable, balanced, and full of good judgment, clear thinking, common sense, reason, experience, and cleverness.

The Mother of Nations is a woman of the Spirit and of the Word. Her life has become conformed to the image of Christ and her heart asks for His will to be done in all things.

Colossians 1:9-12 shows us that we can and should ask for help in this area.

> *For this reason we also, since the day we heard it, do not cease to pray for you, and to ask that you may be filled with the knowledge of His will in all wisdom and spiritual understanding;*
> *That you may walk worthy of the LORD, fully pleasing Him, being fruitful in every work and increasing in the knowledge of God;*
> *Strengthened with all might according to His glorious power, for all patience and long-suffering with joy;*
> *Giving thanks to the Father who has qualified us to be partakers of the inheritance of the saints in the light.*

A Mother of Nations has no problem asking the LORD for wisdom. She is very willing to admit her dependency. James 1:5 assures us, *"If any of you lacks wisdom, let him ask of God, who gives to all liberally and without reproach, and it will be given to him."*

It is important that she asks in faith. She knows that God is the Giver of all wisdom and He desires to impart wisdom to her.

Job and his friends were discussing where wisdom came from in Job 28:12-13.

> *"But where can wisdom be found? And where is the place of understanding?*
> *Man does not know its value, nor is it found in the land of the living."*

Eliphaz, one of Job's comforters, thought wisdom came from observing and experiencing life. He was sure his experiences had made him wise. Bildad, yet another friend of Job's, thought wisdom came from his past, with all its traditions and lessons handed down. He was sure learning from others was the path to become wise. A third friend of Job named Zophar was convinced that only a few had wisdom, and the rest were out of luck. He thought that a person had to figure out who the smart ones were and learn from them.

Job knew there was another source of wisdom. Job saw wisdom as coming from God. To him it was the humble that learned from God, who received God's Word, and obeyed. Job knew man could do a lot, like mine precious ores, make channels in rocks, find facts, create things, and educate himself. But only God is wise. He knew that all wisdom starts with God (Job 28:20-28).

Proverbs 9:10 states, *"The fear of the LORD is the beginning of wisdom."* So the Almighty God, the Creator of heaven and earth, is the source of such divine inspiration.

The woman or man who fears God automatically receives great insight and wisdom from Him.

> *But there is a spirit in man, and the breath of the Almighty gives him understanding.* (Job 32:8)

We are told in Daniel 12:3, *"Those who are wise shall shine like the brightness of the firmament, and those who turn many to righteousness like the stars forever and ever."* Those who have true God-breathed wisdom walk in God's ways, do what He commands, and spend time in His presence continually, trusting and obeying Him. Not only will they shine in the heavenly realm to come, but they shine right here during their earthly sojourn. Jesus even conferred on them the very title He originally bore - "the light of the world" (John 9:5, Matthew 5:14).

Wisdom for a Mother of Nations means that she knows when to make choices, decisions, and changes that benefit the Body of Christ. She has a good understanding of the LORD's will and is willing to do what it takes to accomplish it. I have seen many women over the years face difficult decisions in life. For some it meant major life changes. Those who are spiritually mature have always asked God for wisdom and He has supplied it liberally.

One of the first things God taught me in my early training as a Mother of Nations is that wisdom can come from three sources. The passage that teaches this is James 3:13-17. There is a natural wisdom that comes from education, experience, or listening to and learning from others. There is a demonic inspired wisdom in which evil spirits try to feed you information that appears good, but is actually dark and deadly. Finally, there is godly wisdom that comes from heaven above, straight from the heart and mind of God.

The LORD taught me that God's wisdom is *"first pure, then peaceable, gentle, willing to yield, full of mercy and good fruits, without partiality and without hypocrisy"* (James 3:17).

Both demonic and human wisdom seek their own way, are based in selfish ambition or pride, and bring confusion and every evil thing. They often result in strife, hatred, and contention. In fact, they can make you feel argumentative, agitated, or domineering, driving you to get your way or get your point across. God's wisdom has no hidden agenda, no ego to stroke, no fears to cover up, and no need to promote itself.

God was extremely pleased with Solomon when he requested wisdom. The entire account is well worth reading from 1 Kings 3:4-15.

> *Now the king went to Gibeon to sacrifice there, for that was the great high place: Solomon offered a thousand burnt offerings on that altar.*
>
> *At Gibeon the LORD appeared to Solomon in a dream by night: and God said, "Ask! What shall I give you?"*
>
> *And Solomon said: "You have shown great mercy to Your servant David my father, because he walked before You in truth, in righteousness, and in uprightness of heart with You; You have continued this great kindness for him, and You have given him a son to sit on his throne as it is this day.*
>
> *"Now, O LORD my God, You have made Your servant king instead of my father David, but I am a little child; I do not know how to go out or come in.*

"And Your servant is in the midst of Your people whom You have chosen, a great people, too numerous to be numbered or counted.

"Therefore, give to Your servant an understanding heart to judge Your people, that I may discern between good and evil. For who is able to judge this great people of Yours?"

The speech pleased the LORD, that Solomon had asked this thing.

Then God said to him: "Because you have asked this thing, and have not asked long life for yourself, nor have asked riches for yourself, nor have asked the life of your enemies, but have asked for yourself understanding to discern justice,

"Behold, I have done according to your words; see, I have given you a wise and understanding heart, so that there has not been anyone like you before you, nor shall any like you arise after you.

"And I have also given you what you have not asked; both riches and honor, so that there shall not be anyone like you among the kings all your days.

"So if you walk in My ways, to keep My statutes and My commandments, as your father David walked, then I will lengthen your days."

Then Solomon awoke; and indeed it had been a dream. And he came to Jerusalem and stood before the ark of the covenant of the LORD, offered up burnt offerings, offered peace offerings, and made a feast for all his servants.

Solomon had seen the power of kingship and the need for wisdom. A Mother of Nations knows that she cannot lead or rule without God's wisdom. Proverbs 2:1-11 tells us that the pursuit of wisdom brings security.

> *My son, if you receive my words, and treasure my commands within you,*
>
> *So that you incline your ear to wisdom, and apply your heart to understanding;*
>
> *Yes, if you cry out for discernment, and lift up your voice for understanding,*
>
> *If you seek her as silver, and search for her as for hidden treasures;*
>
> *Then you will understand the fear of the LORD, and find the knowledge of God.*
>
> *For the LORD gives wisdom; from His mouth come knowledge and understanding;*
>
> *He stores up sound wisdom for the upright; He is a shield to those who walk uprightly;*
>
> *He guards the paths of justice, and preserves the way of His saints.*
>
> *Then you will understand righteousness and justice, and equity and every good path.*
>
> *When wisdom enters your heart, and knowledge is pleasant to your soul,*
>
> *Discretion will preserve you; understanding will keep you ....*

If we do not listen to wisdom, we eat the fruit of our own way. Wisdom is the only way to build a house. *"Know also that wisdom is sweet to your soul; if you find it, there is a future hope for you, and your hope will not be cut off"* (Proverbs 24:14 NIV).

The Proverbs 31 woman is certainly a person who seeks this most desirable attribute. In verse 26 of this chapter she is described as *"one who speaks with wisdom and faithful instruction is on her tongue" (NIV)*. The Book of Ecclesiastes lists the many benefits of wisdom. Here are just a few:

Wisdom, like an inheritance, is a good thing and benefits those who see the sun. (Ecclesiastes 7:11 NIV)

Wisdom is a shelter as money is a shelter, but the advantage of knowledge is this: that wisdom preserves the life of its possessor. (Ecclesiastes 7:12 NIV)

Wisdom makes one wise man more powerful than ten rulers in a city. (Ecclesiastes 7:19 NIV)

Wisdom brightens a man's face and changes its hard appearance. (Ecclesiastes 8:1 NIV)

A Mother of Nations realizes that the Spirit of the LORD rests upon her. This includes "*... the Spirit of wisdom and of understanding, the Spirit of counsel and of power, the Spirit of knowledge and the fear of the LORD*" (Isaiah 11:2).

Daniel thanked the LORD for giving him the wisdom and understanding necessary to interpret the king's dream (Daniel 2:23). A Mother of Nations is also grateful to the LORD for the wisdom He has given her to know the plans of her Savior and King. She realizes that not only has He given her the plans, but He has also given her words with such power that none of her opponents or critics are able to withstand them. This truth is found in Jesus' words of Luke 21:15, "*... for I will give you a mouth and wisdom which all your adversaries will not be able to contradict or resist.*"

CHAPTER 10

MOTHERS OF NATIONS
MINISTER IN POWER

"Power will come when the way is paved by prayer."[19]
Harold J. Ockenga,
a leader of 20th Century American Evangelicalism

No Mother of Nations can do all that God has called her to do without His supernatural power at work in her life. In the second chapter of the book of Acts, the power of the Holy Spirit was poured out upon the first century church. From that day on they became witnesses of the LORD Jesus Christ. With God-given power they healed the sick, expelled demons, spoke in tongues, and changed people's lives for all eternity.

This power (*dunamis*—the Greek word from which we derive the terms *dynamic* and *dynamite*) cannot come by education, reading books, or earning degrees. It is not something a woman can buy, manufacture, or create. It is God's gift to be used as He wills. His power and love have been worked into her life so God gets the glory.

God Himself empowers a Mother of Nations with supernatural ability to do what she needs to do. Her source of this power is in Him alone. Psalm 62:11 says, *"God has spoken once. Twice I have heard this: that power belongs to God."* God's power made the earth, redeemed us from our fallen nature, and gave us eternal life. There is God-given power in a Mother of Nation's words, prophecies, prayers, declarations, and decrees.

Over the years we have stood in many countries prophesying the Word of the LORD into those barren lands. At one time Uganda was devastated by a ruthless dictator and ravaged with an epidemic of AIDS. In 1998 seven ladies and I traveled to that nation on an assignment from the LORD. We spoke God's Word into the land with 4,000 leaders agreeing in prayer and declaration. Today Uganda is prospering. We were not the only ones God sent, but as Mothers of Nations, we did our part.

India has also been touched by the power of God. During a recent mission outreach we led over 15,000 people to the LORD in one trip. Over 4,500 women were given Bibles that they too might know the power of God. In Kenya we held a conference with women leaders demonstrating God's power. Many were touched by the LORD and empowered to continue on in their call.

God's power, manifested through a Mother of Nations, casts out devils, breaks curses, heals hearts, and delivers captives. The Bible says in Luke 5:17 that they brought the paralyzed man to Jesus because *"the power of the LORD was present to heal them."*

A Mother of Nations not only has power to help others, but she also has power to help herself. There is power to forgive, power to persevere, power to mature, and power to love. She is not going to yield to jealousy because God has given her security in her own identity and power to trust Him. Possessiveness will not take hold of her because she has the power to release people and things. Fear, anger, rage—all these things may try to take her over, but she has the power to resist.

Mothers of Nations also have power to effectively raise finances for the furtherance of God's purposes. Deuteronomy 8:18 says that God gives us *"power to get wealth."* He wants us to know that His covenant with us is forever and will be established against all odds. When Esther appeared before the King, she went in the power of God. She used her natural abilities as well as God's power. Today the Jews celebrate Purim, which is a celebration of the power of God working on behalf of His people. This celebration dates back to the time of Esther.

In the New Testament Luke 10:19 tells us that God gives us authority and power to trample on serpents and scorpions. Then Jesus added that we have power over all the power of the enemy and nothing shall by any means hurt us. The devil cannot win when a Mother of Nations knows her position, power, and authority in Christ.

Every aspiring Mother of Nations should remind herself often of the following identity truths:

- She is a child of God (John 1:12).

- She is a friend of God (John 15:15).

- She is a saint (Ephesians 1:1).

- She is a temple of God (1 Corinthians 6:19-20).

- She has been adopted by God (Ephesians 1:5-6).

- She has direct access to God (Ephesians 2:18).

- She cannot be separated from the love of God (Romans 8:35-39).

- She is a citizen of heaven (Philippians 3:20).

- She is the salt of the earth (Matthew 5:13).

- She is the light of the world (Matthew 5:14).

- She is chosen and appointed to bear fruit (John 15:16).

- She is God's co-worker (1 Corinthians 3:9).

- She is a member of a chosen race (1 Peter 2:9 Amp).

- She is part of a royal priesthood (1 Peter 2:9).

- She is an enemy of the devil (1 Peter 5:8).

- She has the mind of Christ (1 Corinthians 2:16).

The Mother of Nations has learned from experience and knows how to walk in the supernatural power of God as a lifestyle. She is fully aware that there is no greater power or authority anywhere in this world. No wonder such powerful history-makers are referred to in Hannah's prophetic song as *"pillars of the earth"* (1 Samuel 2:8).

CHAPTER 11

MOTHERS OF NATIONS
ARE LOVE-BEINGS

"Before we can minister in love,
we must be mastered by love."
Unknown Author

Whenever I hear a song with a theme of our calling to the nations, I start to get emotional and cry. My heart begins to enlarge, to swell with feelings of love and longing to go to the nations and bring God's love to the masses of people who are in such need of this revelation. At first I thought I was just being overly emotional or sensitive, but as the years have gone by, the feelings have deepened and the tears have increased. They are not only a result of the burden I bear, but recognition of the price others are paying or have paid. It is also a sensing of the heartbeat of God for people. Jesus paid with His life so that we might be saved. God's love was so great that no sacrifice was too big. He was willing to pay the most overwhelming price of all in giving His own Son for us to be cleansed of sin.

Love is sacrificial. It is a willingness to give, as well as a willingness to do whatever we can to help mankind. *"For anyone who does not love his brother, whom he has seen, cannot love God, whom he has not seen. And He has given us this command: whoever loves God must also love his brother"* (1 John 4:20-21 NIV).

God is saying in His Word that true love is expressed and demonstrated in loving others. The Word commands us to first love God, next ourselves, and then others. Our love toward God should be complete, consuming our body, soul, and spirit. His love in us gives us a love toward ourselves and a love toward other people for He has created us all in His image.

> *This is how we know what love is: Jesus Christ laid down His life for us. And we ought to lay down our lives for our brothers.* (1 John 3:16 NIV)

Love is the giving of oneself, whether it is one's life, one's goods, or one's rights. With all the issues in the world today, the expression of God's love is found in trying to meet those needs and problems.

Mothers of Nations find themselves giving away clothes to the poor, making blankets for those who have none, buying toys for orphans, and sending bicycles to ministers in foreign lands. I have seen many women over the years put on garage sales, bake sales, jewelry sales, and the like to raise funds for the poor. Some have sponsored golf outings to raise funds. Others have sacrificed their income tax returns and savings to help educate a child or feed a family. On my last trip to India a woman pastor came with me. When she saw there was a need for sewing machines, the first thing that she volunteered to do was to go back home and raise funds for those machines. That was a demonstration of a mother's love!

Romans 5:8 explains that *"God demonstrates His own love toward us, in that while we were still sinners, Christ died for us."* So God showed His magnanimous kindness and compassion toward us by giving the gift of all gifts. He offered His own Son as the avenue for salvation to mankind. God gave to us so that we in turn would give to others. With that gift comes life, healing, deliverance, restoration, redemption, justification, sanctification, cleansing from unrighteousness, eternal life, and so much more.

A Mother of Nations is a love-being. She is a lover of mankind, compassionate, and kind. She carries love in her heart to distribute to the nations in the earth. Her love is constant, voluntary, and surprising to many. Who can understand the love of a mother? Psalm 2:8 tells us to ask for the nations as our inheritance and that is exactly what a Mother of Nations does. She asks for the nations out of her love for them. This love comes from the Father above who instills in her, by the cross of Calvary and the calling of the Holy Spirit, a deep, abiding love for all races, genders, and ages. She knows no boundaries when it comes to God's love for the nations.

I have been with women called to nations who will get down in the dirt to pray for a child, eat the most unappetizing food, or travel miles just to express God's love to a few people. This love God has placed in their hearts for mankind propels them to do all they can to reach people with the Gospel message. A Mother of Nations does not love because she feels someone deserves it, nor does she love out of pity. She loves because God's love has been shed abroad in her heart by the Holy Spirit (Romans 5:5).

The Bible tells us of many instances in which Jesus was moved by compassion. Compassion is the deep feeling of sharing the suffering of another, together with the inclination to give aid, lend support, or show mercy. Out of Jesus' compassion flowed healing, deliverance, and benevolence to His fellow man. Paul told the Galatian church that *"faith works through love"* (Galatians 5:6). A Mother of Nations, flowing in the anointing of love, reaches out with God's Word and Spirit to bring healing and deliverance.

Mothers of Nations also know the power of love expressed through forgiveness. Unforgiving persons desire restitution, justice, revenge, apologies, or some form of proof that they were slighted or mistreated. They become critical of people, scheming, and angry. A Mother of Nations, operating in love, sees both sides of the coin. She understands differences of opinion, doctrine, religious bondage, the times, and the cultural beliefs of a nation. She is not quick to judge or condemn, but rather, she is quick to learn and to forgive. Her love is expressed through her own understanding of the sinful nature of human beings and her own need for salvation. She desires for all people to be free. Forgiveness in her heart keeps her and others free from having to pay restitution or be under obligation.

In our cruel world, parents often withdraw love when their children do not perform according to their standards or expectations. Mothers of Nations go to the other extreme, giving people grace, time to change, and the opportunity to discover God's love along the way.

Loving others means we smile more, encourage more, and learn to come alongside as a supporter rather than an accuser. When we go on a mission outreach we are always careful not to evaluate a foreigner's methods by our American culture or ways. Love realizes that there are many expressions of faith in life. There are many demonstrations of love, and some cultures do not desire or need our American traditions such as Christmas gifts or Easter baskets. Love accepts their choice of refusing cultural trends that give rise to materialism or class division because some have money for gifts and some do not. When we are operating in a forgiving heart, it means we choose to love our enemies, bless those who curse us, do good to those who hate us, and pray for those who persecute us. In doing so Jesus said, *"You shall be perfect, just as your Father in heaven is perfect"* (Matthew 5:48).

I once heard an inspirational story about two brothers who aspired to be artists. The famous "Praying Hands" picture was created by one these brothers, Albrecht Durer (1471-1528). Born in Germany, the son of a Hungarian goldsmith, "Albert," as he was called, and his brother were studying art together. However, the meager income they made on the side didn't even provide for their bare necessities. They decided to take turns supporting each other. One would work while the other studied, then they would switch.

Albert became a skilled artist while his brother worked in a dangerous mine to pay their bills. Finally the day arrived when Albert would begin working while his brother pursued his artistic dreams. Sadly, as a result of hard manual labor, the brother's hands were so battered and swollen he could no longer hold a brush steady enough to paint. His career as an artist was over. Disappointed by his brother's fate, Albert returned to their room one day to find him praying with his hands held in a reverent prayer posture. Instantly Albert was inspired to create the picture of the "praying hands." The brother's lost skill could never be restored but it could be memorialized through this picture. It expressed his love and appreciation for the sacrificial labor his friend had performed. Albert hoped that his painting would inspire viewers to show selfless love to others.

Those beautiful praying hands are what we often see depicted in art, on note cards, and in porcelain images and sculpture. One brother's love was expressed in his art and the other brother's love expressed in his sacrificial labor. What a compelling story of love! One worked and one learned, yet both did something to change the world.

That is exactly how I see a Mother of Nations. She is one who shows love to the world by sacrificing her time, energy, and heart for others. Some Mothers of Nations work to raise funds for the foreign or local mission while others go out to the field and reach the lost. Paul made this distinction in Romans 10:14-15, " ... *And how shall they hear without a preacher? And how shall they preach unless they are sent?"* Clearly some are specifically called by God to take the Gospel message, while others are called by God to financially and prayerfully support those who go.

Perfect love is manifested in forgiveness. It is also sacrificial and it "casts out fear" (1 John 4:18). The Mother of Nations cannot operate in love for nations and walk in fear simultaneously. Fear can come through the anticipation of a problem, rejection, failure, disease, lack of acceptance, criticism, or death. But love says, "I can trust God." Rejection based in fear is something everyone faces at some point or another. People may like you one day and dislike you the next. Rejection can come from some of the people you try to help the most. It can come from family members who resent your authority, or an unspiritual spouse who resents the depth of your spirituality or is upset with you because of an unwanted pregnancy.

Rejection can result from jealousy over your appearance, your status in life, or simply the way that other people bless you. Joseph's brothers hated him and rejected him, not because of anything *he did*, but because of what *others did for him* (the dreams that God gave him and the coat that his father gave him). At times rejection comes because carnal-minded people resent your "coat of many colors" too - your anointing and the favor of God that rests upon you.

A Mother of Nations, walking and abiding in love, overcomes rejection by forgiving those who reject her. She gives the problem to Jesus and accepts the truth that no matter what, God loves her. Her role model is Jesus. Jesus disregarded the rejection of people by realizing that they were really rejecting the One who sent Him. He was very bold in proclaiming *"that all should honor the Son just as they honor the Father."* Then He drove the point home even further saying, *"He who does not honor the Son does not honor the Father who sent Him"* (John 5:23).

Jesus chose to stay in the Father's love even when many people rejected His teaching and refused to accept that He was the promised Messiah. Outside the Garden of Gethsemane He focused, not on the detractors denouncing Him, but on the disciples devoted to Him, when He interceded, *"Father ... I do not pray for the world, but for those whom You have given Me ... I have declared to them Your name, and will declare it, that the love with which You loved Me may be in them, and I in them"* (John 17:1, 9, 26).

Mothers of Nations disregard rejection and see it as a rejection of Jesus. They remember His words, *"He who hears you hears Me, he who rejects you rejects Me, and he who rejects Me rejects Him who sent Me"* (Luke 10:16). They stay secure in God's love for them and focus their attention instead on those who are receptive to Christ, pouring out God's love on them.

The last thing a Mother of Nations should ever do is turn to anger, criticism, rebellion, self-pity, or mistrust. This behavior gives too much power to others and diminishes her own. Her heart is to be secure in how God feels about her. Her mindset is to love at all times, even when she is not loved in return.

We hosted a missionary to the Philippines at our church one time who told of a torturous situation he experienced. Terrorists had captured him and were tormenting him.

One of the leaders was a corrupt Catholic priest who was an undercover Marxist-Communist. The priest put a tube in the missionary's mouth and filled him with water. Then they put electrical cords to his body and shocked him. As the torture took place, the Holy Spirit kept telling the missionary to tell the priest that He loved him. The tortured man could not bring himself to say these words from his heart. He wrestled with the thought until he finally said it. The priest, shocked by the words "I love you," stopped the torture and said that is enough. They left the missionary for dead. Fortunately, he was able to find his way to safety and eventually made it home. It was the power of those words of love that broke the shackles. God's love is so powerful that even the worst criminal can be touched by it. God's love can soften the hardest heart.

A Mother of Nations loves. She knows God has made a covenant of love with her for all eternity. What does God require of her but to fear the LORD her God, to walk in all His ways, and to love Him. She will serve the LORD her God with all her heart and all her soul because she operates in a divine love this world cannot comprehend.

CHAPTER 12

MOTHERS OF NATIONS
ARE PRAYER WARRIORS

"Work as if everything depends on you
and pray as if everything depends on God."[20]
William Booth, founder of the Salvation Army

Prayer is the lifestyle of a Mother of Nations. It is one thing you will not find lacking in her life. She knows that prayer is partnering with the Holy Spirit to make things happen in the heavens and on the earth. Prayer not only advances God's Kingdom, but it also influences man's kingdoms. Her prayers are more focused on others than herself.

Prayer is intimacy with God. We communicate with God through prayer. Whether it is praying in the Spirit, asking for help, or thanking God, we are communicating with our Father. Jesus communicated with His Father before making major decisions. Sometimes that meant praying all night. Matthew 14:23 reminds us, *"And when He had sent the multitudes away, He went up into a mountain apart to pray; and when the evening was come, He was there alone."*

A Mother of Nations does not see her prayer life as something to display or brag about. Her walk with God is intimate and private. Jesus taught the disciples to see the difference between a public display of prayer and heartfelt prayer as described in Matthew 6:5-6.

"And when you pray, you shall not be like the hypocrites. For they love to pray standing in the synagogues and on the corners of the streets, that they may be seen by men. Assuredly, I say to you, they have their reward.

But you, when you pray, go into your room, and when you have shut your door, pray to your Father who is in the secret place; and your Father who sees in secret will reward you openly."

Mothers of Nations will find themselves praying just like Jesus did. He prayed for children to be blessed, for Peter not to fall prey to the devil, and for healing and deliverance to many. He prayed so often and so well that His disciples asked Him to teach them how to pray (Luke 11:1). A Mother of Nations should be known as a woman of prayer and be able to teach others to pray as well. She might find herself in a similar position as Abraham who was called on by God to intercede for a wicked region where some of his family members lived. God knew if he told Abraham about His plans to destroy Sodom and Gomorrah, Abraham would pray (Genesis 18). His intercession proved to be invaluable. Though those infamous cities were not spared because they lacked enough righteous inhabitants, Abraham's nephew and his family were spared. The Bible explains:

God remembered Abraham, and sent Lot out of the midst of the overthrow, when He overthrew the cities in which Lot had dwelt. (Genesis 19:29)

Many people have a prayer life, but a Mother of Nations lives in prayer. Her spirit is always attentive to the Holy Spirit that she might obey His call to pray.

We have been on mission trips when the Holy Spirit suddenly prompted us to "Pray." For instance, in Kenya I once heard the Holy Spirit say, "Worship right now!" It was a type of intercessory prayer. I commanded everyone to immediately worship and pray. Right after that moment, what looked like a ghost appeared on the road that we were traveling. The spirit, appearing in the form of a female ghost, wearing a long, flowing blue gown, was hovering a few inches off the ground and walking down the middle of the road. The driver swerved to miss her, only to realize it was only an apparition. We found out later that many people had died in car accidents on that road due to these phantom-like beings appearing at night. Drivers, thinking these apparitions were real people, swerved to avoid them and ended up in the ditch. Obeying the immediate call to pray helped us evade disaster.

A Mother of Nations knows how and when to pray. She has a prayer partner in her life because like Paul, she is a "partner with God." She knows how to cooperate with God. The God of Abraham has always desired that His people have access into His presence. Even under the Old Will, when He brought them out of Egypt He announced, " ... *Although the whole earth is Mine, you will be for Me a kingdom of priests*" (Exodus 19:5-6 NIV). In other words, out of all the nations you will be unique, a nation of people who have the right to prayerfully draw near to the true God to minister to Him. Not only are Mothers of Nations partners, they are priests of God as well. Actually, according to 1 Peter 2:5 and 9, all believers are called *"a holy priesthood"* and *"a royal priesthood."*

The prayer life of a Mother of Nations is filled with power to resist and power to defeat the devil. The devil comes and tries to steal, kill, and destroy, but the Mother of Nations knows how to stand firm in her faith. She takes hold of the promises of God, prays for angelic assistance, and cancels the devil's assignment. Whether she is on the mission field or at home, this woman can get through to God in prayer. It does not matter if it is individual prayer, corporate prayer, intercessory prayer, short prayers or long, she can reach that place in prayer that few can attain. This is that secret place in God where His secrets are revealed and revelation knowledge flows.

Prayer is a matter of heart, not just words. It is a demonstration of our dependency upon God. I once read a statement that said, "prayerlessness is arrogance." I thought, "Wow, how true!" It is humility that causes one to pray. With the heart of a warrior, who abides in humble submission to the Captain of her salvation, the Mother of Nations becomes a support to others through her prayer lifestyle.

Mothers of Nations model their prayer lives after other Biblical leaders. Job continually offered burnt sacrifices to intercede on behalf of his children (Job 1:5). David prayed that he could keep his heart right before God. Solomon prayed for wisdom and good leadership skills. Daniel asked Hananiah, Mishael, and Azariah to pray that God would reveal to him the nature and interpretation of the king's dream. Paul asked others to pray that doors of opportunity for him to preach would open. He also asked for zeal and love in his ministry. The list goes on. Each one needed and requested help through prayer.

When we pray like a Mother of Nations, we are sensitive to the needs of others.

It is our way of consigning ourselves to the role of servants, for our primary focus becomes the betterment of those we can influence. 1 Corinthians 9:19-20, 22 tells us:

> *For though I be free from all men, yet have I made myself servant unto all that I might gain the more.*
>
> *And unto the Jews I became as a Jew, that I might gain the Jews; to them that are under the law, as under the law, that I might gain them that are under the law ….*
>
> *To the weak became I as weak, that I might gain the weak; I am made all things to all men, that I might by all means save some.*

We are to fight for others by binding the forces that bind them. We engage in battle for them and cannot quit until we complete our assignment. We aim our prayer weapons at the target. We pull up the roots of the enemy until we get to the core problem.

Prayer in a Mother of Nation's life means sacrifice. She may be called to pray at the midnight hour. She may be asked to fast or be requested by the Holy Spirit to pray for days, months, or even years, concerning a specific cause or purpose. Every day her time, plans, and schedule have to be given over to the LORD. She never knows what the LORD may ask her to do. All she knows is obedience is better than sacrifice and that God will give her grace to complete any task to which she is assigned.

My first introduction to a life of prayer came right after I had received the power of the Holy Spirit's baptism. Hungry for God, I was continually looking for meetings to attend where I could learn more about the things of the LORD. One night I went to a Women's Aglow meeting, on the third floor of a hotel, where a powerfully anointed woman was preaching on intercession in the life of Moses and Abraham. At the end of her message she gave an altar call for all those called to be intercessors. Not fully understanding the call, or even the definition of an intercessor, I left the meeting and went down three floors, then proceeded outside to the parking lot of another building. The moment I put my key into the car door an audible voice said, "Get back up there." It wasn't quiet, rather loud, clear, and commanding. I thought for sure everyone in the parking lot had heard it, but as I looked around, no one was paying attention.

Immediately I realized I was hearing the audible voice of God. I ran back to the building, up those three flights of stairs, and into the meeting room. With such a feeling of urgency and obedience, I walked right up to the speaker and said, "Pray for me!" Instantly as she laid her hand on me, I fell over under the power of the Holy Spirit and started speaking in tongues. That night as I drove home I continued speaking in tongues. As I tried to fall asleep I couldn't because my prayer language kept changing from one dialect to another. I am sure I prayed in over thirty languages, if not more, as I envisioned the globe and me traveling the world. It was my first all night prayer vigil!

The next day at noon I felt an urge to pray and so I yielded to that pull, again praying strong and in tongues. This call to prayer around noon continued daily for almost the next year and a half. I would lie on my side and groan in the Spirit. Other times I would stand up and declare God's Word as He gave the words to me. I would bind and loose and just do whatever God said to do as I prayed.

Because these experiences were so new to me, I became concerned if I might be getting off-balance in my spiritual experience. I talked to others who were older believers and they said that yes, they had experienced such callings to prayer, but only once or twice in their lives. I was feeling this call to pray daily! I was becoming concerned, so I asked the Holy Spirit to teach me exactly what was happening to me.

The next week I was in a Christian bookstore and was browsing through a shelf with books on the topic of prayer. I pulled a book titled Praying Hyde and took it home to read. As I studied that book I knew that I had received an answer from the LORD regarding my prayer experiences and that I was being led by HIM to pray.

Several weeks into my "afternoon prayer times" I started getting the scripture Jeremiah 33 in my spirit. Some days

I would pray only ten minutes, others I might pray two or three hours. Each day I prayed until I felt the prompting of the Holy Spirit lift, but at the end of those prayer times He would always encourage me to read Jeremiah 33.

Jeremiah 33 used to be such a puzzle to me. Why would God lead me to read that chapter every day at the end of my prayer time? This went on for one and a half years! I asked pastors and leaders to explain Jeremiah 33 to me. Books, commentaries, encyclopedias, and anything I could find were searched and read. Nothing satisfied my hunger nor seemed to explain the chapter to me. Finally after six years passed, I gave up my investigation and concluded that I would never know why I had prayed that chapter so often.

Then in 1985 my pastor at that time asked me to go to India with her on a mission trip. Through some extenuating circumstances she was unable to go, so my husband came along with me instead. As part of our itinerary we went to visit a Christian school started by Dr. Chacko Varghese in Cochin, India, called Peniel Bible College. *Peniel* means "face of God" or "encounter with God" as found in Genesis 32:30. There on the campus each day I would hear the students in the college come out of their rooms singing, worshipping God, and sounding so happy. There were sounds of joy and gladness everywhere, even as they worked they sang.

About four days after being on the school grounds, my husband and I were asked to speak at the graduation service and to testify of the LORD's blessings. Sitting on the stage and listening to the president of the Assemblies of God in India, someone decided to interpret his message for us. As the interpretation was given to us of the stages of building the college, I recognized that Peniel Bible College was the manifestation of my Jeremiah 33 experiences!

Overwhelmed by this realization, I began to understand that God had made it possible for me to come all the way to India to be part of this. Then, like a Father handing his child a gift, God Himself was unveiling before my eyes my life of prayer and what had happened as a result of it. Those eighteen months of prayer in my Minnesota bedroom had birthed Peniel Bible College in India! As Jeremiah 33 said, it was a desolate place, a place that had sinned and had been inhabited by demons, but God had come and cleansed the land. It was now a place of great singing and joy. Here are some of the key verses in that chapter (verses 10-12):

> *"Thus says the LORD: 'Again there shall be heard in this place—of which you say, "It is desolate, without man and without beast"—in the cities of Judah, in the streets of Jerusalem that are desolate, without man and without inhabitant and without beast,*
>
> *The voice of joy and the voice of gladness, the voice of the bridegroom and the voice of the bride, the voice of those who will say: "Praise the LORD of hosts, For the LORD is good, For His mercy endures forever"— and of those who will bring the sacrifice of praise into the house of the LORD. For I will cause the captives of the land to return as at the first,' says the LORD.*
>
> *"Thus says the LORD of hosts: 'In this place which is desolate, without man and without beast, and in all its cities, there shall again be a dwelling place of shepherds causing their flocks to lie down.'"*

There are no words to explain the feelings I experienced that day as I realized that God did not just want to tell me about my Jeremiah 33 prayers, but He wanted to show me. My heart was so overwhelmed by this experience that I could not even speak. I realized that my bedroom prayer had impacted a nation! I had been obedient to pray as the Holy

Spirit led me, but completely unaware of the higher purpose of it all.

Unknowingly, I had birthed a Bible school in my prayer closet and paved the way to send shepherds out into the field where there were no shepherds. Today Peniel Bible College of Cochin, India, sends men and women into many areas of India to start churches and bring the Gospel to the other surrounding nations.

Jabez prayed a prayer that every Mother of Nations needs to know; he pled:

"Oh, that You would bless me indeed, and enlarge my territory, that Your hand would be with me, and that You would keep me from evil, that I may not cause pain!" (1 Chronicles 4:10)

Jabez was actually asking to have a greater influence for God. He wanted to live beyond the natural limits he knew. He wanted God's full blessing and favor so his cup would run over. Jabez wanted God's plan, knowing it would be better and more rewarding than his own agenda. He wanted his life to be a blessing to many and to make a difference. He asked that he would be kept from evil and never bring harm to anyone.

What a powerful prayer! Like Jabez, the Mother of Nation's heart is to bless and never to harm anyone. Enlargement in her ministry means to further the Kingdom of God and expand its reach through her life. More than once we have been in foreign countries where we have prayed for leaders of that country. We have prayed for the Minister of Power in India, the Minister of Ethics and Integrity in Uganda, the President of an Asian country and his Prime Minister, plus many more. Even movie stars and celebrities have requested prayer from our ministry. A Mother of Nations will pray for people in all walks of life. No one is more important to her than another, for truly, there is no respect of persons in Christ. The poor and the rich, the uneducated and the highly educated, the common and the famous, they are all equally important in the sight of God and to be treated with dignity. However, she must also recognize the importance of ministering to leaders (political, social and religious) because through them a far greater number of people can be influenced for the sake of the truth.

Satan understands this principle in its negative application. That's why he went after Peter to sift him as wheat. He knew Peter was a natural born leader, anointed for a chief role in the soon-to-be-born fledging church. The devil also knew that if he could sway Peter, he could sway the many thousands who would eventually come under his apostolic anointing and ministry. That's why Jesus paid particular attention in intercession to his chief apostle, warning and promising:

" ... *Simon, Simon, behold, Satan has desired you, that he may sift you as wheat. But I have prayed for you, that your faith fail not.*" (Luke 22:31-32)

Jesus knew, as the Apostle and High Priest of our profession, that His intercessory appeal to the Father would make a difference in Peter's future destiny. A Mother of Nations needs to recognize that her prayers are important as well. Her petitions can help to undergird and shape the destiny of those affected by her ministry, even leaders and entire nations. She must view herself as a nation-builder, ready to prayerfully influence key national leaders and thereby, impact the nations under their charge for the glory of God. Yet all the while, she must be sensitive to the importance of each individual in the sight of heaven.

Whether it is intimacy with the LORD, identifying with a person's problems, or agonizing over the pain of others, a Mother of Nations will arise to the task. She is willing to bear burdens and pray them through until there is a breakthrough.

Lastly, the Mother of Nations prays the heart of God. How does she know His heart? By listening to the Spirit's voice and yielding to His influence. God has a global vision of the reacquisition of this planet. A Mother of Nations senses the enormous responsibility that rests upon her to help in this process.

The following passages of Scripture teach us that God's heart is to impact, not just individuals but entire nations and regions. We must understand that collectively the earth is our charge and we must all take personal responsibility for it. Psalm 115:16 says, *"The heaven, even the heavens, are the LORD's; But the earth He has given to the children of men."* As you read these passages about the Creator's dominion reaching around the world, keep in mind John Wesley's observation that *"God does nothing except in response to believing prayer."*

> *Declare His glory among the nations; His wonders among all peoples.* (1 Chronicles 16:24)

> *Let the heavens rejoice, and let the earth be glad and let them say among the nations, "the LORD reigns."* (1 Chronicles 16:31)

> *All the ends of the world shall remember and turn to the LORD, and all the families of the nations shall worship before You.* (Psalm 22:27)

> *For the kingdom is the LORD'S and He rules the nations.* (Psalm 22:28)

That Your way may be known upon the earth, Your salvation among all nations. (Psalm 67:2)

Many nations shall come and say, "Come, let us go up to the mountain of the LORD, to the house of the God of Jacob, He will teach us His ways ...." (Micah 4:2)

"And this Gospel of the kingdom shall be preached in all the world for a witness unto all nations, and then the end will come." (Matthew 24:14)

CHAPTER 13

MOTHERS OF NATIONS EXPECT EXCELLENCE

"Excellence is never cheap. It is costly.
Constant care, serious preparation, and
continual application are required.
Excellence involves desire
plus discipline plus determination."[21]
Dr. George Sweeting,
former president of Moody Bible Institute

In Ruth 3:11 we find Boaz assuring Ruth that he would perform the duty of a nearest kinsman by marrying her. His words were surely a comfort to her.

"And now my daughter, fear not: I will do to you all
that you require: for all the city of my people does know
that you are a virtuous woman."

Other versions quote him describing her as *"a woman of strength (worth, bravery, capability)"*—*"a worthy woman"*—*"a woman of good character"* (Amp, ASV, CJB). In other words, Ruth was recognized throughout the city of Bethlehem as a woman of excellence. You cannot be an excellent woman without having excellent ways.

The name *Ruth* means "friendship." She was a true friend to Naomi when her mother-in-law was an elderly woman and needed her companionship. Evidently Ruth valued loyalty above her own personal well-being. When she and her sister-in-law Orpah were given an opportunity to leave Naomi (because their husbands, Naomi's sons, had died), Ruth responded,

"Entreat me not to leave you, or to turn back from following after you; for wherever you go, I will go; and wherever you lodge, I will lodge; your people shall be my people, and your God, my God.

Where you die, I will die, and there will I be buried. The LORD *do so to me, and more also, If anything but death parts you and me."* (Ruth 1:16-17)

What an excellent heart! Orpah left Naomi and went her way. Even though leaving could have meant a far better situation for Ruth, she remained. Being a true friend and abiding in a covenant relationship meant much more to her than having an easier life.

The word excellent means "first-rate, top-notch, premium, of the highest quality, exceptional, admirable, and the best." All of these definitions are good ways of describing this unique Biblical character.

Scripture seems to indicate that Ruth lived in a time when many people were doing what was right in their own eyes instead of God's. Yet she shined in the midst of such darkness as someone of worth, a person of real excellence. Ruth was exactly what her name implied: a true friend to her mother-in-law Naomi, to the God of Abraham, and to all who were touched by her life. The "real thing" is not always easy to find.

Women called to be Mothers of Nations are women of such excellence that others take notice. Ruth made a commitment and all her family members and the people in the city saw her keep it. Her heart was willing to serve Naomi, obey her counsel, and trust her as she followed her to a strange place. Ruth had lost her husband, her source of income, and her land, yet she remained faithful to the one who needed her.

Caught in widowhood, Ruth was willing to go to the fields and glean ears of corn. A woman engaged in such activity could have easily flirted with the workers to get more grain, but not Ruth. Integrity ruled her conduct. Because of her outstanding willingness to serve, she found herself in the right field at exactly the right time. That was no mere coincidence, but was surely the hand of divine providence!

Humble and diligent, Ruth ended up in the field of her master, right where he could see her and become familiar with her ways. She was not moving from field to field, but she chose to stay in the one the LORD, through Naomi, had directed her to work. Mothers of Nations labor in the field where God puts them. They are not church-hoppers or church-shoppers. Wherever God places them at the beginning, they stay until the field has been harvested to the Master's satisfaction. Mothers of Nations, trained to walk in excellence, have learned to be still.

Ruth 3:16-18 declares:

> *When she came to her mother-in-law, she said, "Is that you, my daughter?" Then she told her all that the man had done for her.*
>
> *And she said, "These six ephahs of barley he gave me; for he said to me, Do not go empty-handed to your mother-in-law."*
>
> *Then she said, "Sit still, my daughter, until you know how the matter will turn out; for the man will not rest until he has concluded the matter this day."*

Naomi told Ruth to sit still until she knew how the situation would end. We must trust God to finish the work He has started in us. Ruth did exactly as Naomi said and she ended up marrying Boaz. In one of the most remarkable stories of redemption, Ruth, an impoverished widow, was married by her kinsman redeemer Boaz. Together they had a son named Obed, who in turn had a son named Jesse, who later had a son named David. So, through a miraculous series of events, Ruth became the great-grandmother of David, the King of Israel. Blessings came to her and Naomi because she chose the path of excellence.

An "excellent spirit" dwells in a Mother of Nations just like it did in Daniel. Daniel was isolated from his family, indoctrinated with heathen knowledge, tempted continually by others to compromise, and forced to change his godly name to a heathen one. Yet Daniel purposed in his heart to give God his best. Excellence to him was the only choice. In fact, he was preferred above all the other presidents and princes of Babylon because *an excellent spirit was in him*" (Daniel 6:3). Daniel rose from being a prisoner of war (a captive in a strange land) to being a chief ruler of the Babylonian Empire due to the favor of God and his passionate pursuit of excellence.

Mothers of Nations demonstrate their excellence in their values and ideals. They always raise up a godly standard for others to follow. Their lives are lived to glorify God by excelling more. They choose to fill their minds with thoughts of success and victory. Dissatisfied with mediocrity, they are motivated to pursue something higher called "excellence." Paul called it *the mark for the prize of the high calling of God in Christ Jesus*" (Philippians 3:14). A Mother of Nations will not leave a ministry the way she first found it. She will do her best to improve it, develop it, and see it grow, giving glory to God and touching many lives for Christ.

A Mother of Nations realizes that people often resist change, but she is not deterred. Her passion for excellence and for the achieving of her highest potential far exceeds her desire to be accepted by those who do not share similar aspirations. When opposition comes, she does not allow resentment and anger to take hold of her heart. She merely keeps her sights high, realizing that not all will follow her, but some will—and for their sakes she continues.

Because of her striving for excellence, a Mother of Nations can bring an end to curses and start a line of blessing. The Moabites were a cursed people (Deuteronomy 23:1-5). God said they would never come into the assembly of His people because the King of Moab did not meet the children of Israel with bread and water when they came out of Egypt, but hired Balaam to pronounce a curse on them. But Ruth's heart so captured the heart of God that He cancelled an irreversible curse just for her sake.

Then, most amazingly, God positioned Ruth as a matriarch in a family line that would bring forth royal seed in Israel, culminating in the birth of the Messiah Himself. In a way she never could have imagined possible, she truly became a Mother of Nations in a long-term sense, because by the end of this age, every nation will be impacted by the Gospel of the LORD Jesus Christ and the revelation of the Kingdom of God.

One woman, striving for excellence, became an integral part of a divine plan that spanned both the Old and New Covenant eras. If you receive this call, you will probably never know the full importance and impact of your life.

CHAPTER 14

MOTHERS OF NATIONS
ARE PROPHETIC IN NATURE

"And it shall come to pass in the last days, says God,
That I will pour out of My Spirit on all flesh;
Your sons and your daughters shall prophesy ...."
(Acts 2:17)

Prophets are uniquely designed and developed by God. Mothers of Nations may not be prophets in the highest sense, although many are, but they will all be prophetically inclined. To prophesy doesn't just involve foretelling or predicting the future. It can simply be a forth telling, proclaiming the truth in a direct, authoritative way, speaking God's Word under the inspiration of the Holy Spirit. Like Elijah and John the Baptist, Mothers of Nations will be sent to a people group with the Word of the LORD. God's thoughts and future plans will be in their heart for the nations in which they minister.

Prophets spend intimate time with the LORD seeking His face. God said in His Word that if there are prophets among us, He will make Himself known to them in visions and dreams (Numbers 12:6). Mothers of Nations, having spent time with God, are solely devoted to Him and know His purposes. They have a direct communication system with God. At times they receive inspired dreams and visions from the Almighty.

Some are friends of God like Abraham (James 2:23). Similar to this great patriarch, they have a very trusting heart regarding their Father. They converse back and forth, discussing His plans and praying for them to come to pass.

In the New Testament the LORD calls His chief disciples (who were all apostolic and prophetic in their callings) *"His friends"* (John 15:15). He explained that this was so because all that the Father had revealed to Him, He in turn had transferred to them. The Mother of Nations is a friend of God and He speaks profound things to her heart.

Amos 3:7 states, *"Surely the LORD God does nothing, unless He reveals His secret to His servants the prophets."* Receiving His message, they either pray that word through until it happens or they are the faithful messengers who deliver it. Mothers of Nations go and tell. They are sent to nations, cities, tribes, leaders, churches, and individuals. Choosing to be bond slaves with no rights of their own, they serve the LORD by choice. Mothers of Nations know that bond slaves do what the Master asks voluntarily, without question or excuse.

In ancient times watchmen positioned themselves in high towers on the walls of the cities for which they were responsible. They would gaze through a hole or a slot in the turret to see if an enemy was approaching. They had to remain alert and attentive all the time. I see Mothers of Nations as watchmen (or watchwomen) who remain alert to the Holy Spirit and attentive to His requests. These women are awake while others might be sleeping spiritually. There are plenty of examples in Scripture.

- Miriam, the sister of Moses, led the women of Israel in dancing and singing as she recognized the greatness of the miracle God had just wrought in overthrowing the Egyptian army.

- Deborah was alert to the day of salvation in Israel; she knew when to go to war.

- Anna, the prophetess, was alert to the coming of the

Messiah and was attentive in the sanctuary waiting for Him.

- Mary was alert enough to sit at the feet of Jesus and listen to His wisdom, even though she was misjudged and derided by her sister Martha, who thought she should be working.

When prophets come into our midst, we see influence at work. Their requests, or sometimes even demands, are met by others. People may resist at first but usually the prophet gets results.

We see the example in Scripture where Elijah asked a widow woman to bake him a cake of bread in the time of famine. She resisted at first. It meant major sacrifice and an uncertain future. It was her last bit of meal and she planned on cooking it for herself and her son and then would both die. But the prophet knew her obedience to him meant a better life for her. He prophesied and it came to pass, *"the bin of flour was not used up, nor did the jar of oil run dry, according to the word of the LORD"* until the LORD sent rain on the earth (1 Kings 17:16). Elijah was willing to press the issue for her sake.

Later, when her son became ill, she saw it as a punishment from God. In anger and resentment she cried out to Elijah, *"What have I to do with you, O man of God? Have you come to me to bring my sin to remembrance, and to kill my son?"* (1 Kings 17:18) She blamed Elijah for the problem when he was actually the solution to the problem, for it was through Elijah that her son was raised from the dead.

This kind of false accusation happens often. Mothers of Nations may prophetically help someone, even save that person's life, but may be mocked, ridiculed, or even hated in return. A Mother of Nations will not take offense, but rather will cry out to the LORD for those who offend. She does not take on a person's fear or panic. Instead, she distances herself from the negativity of weak or carnal minded believers. Rising above the circumstances, she responds in compassion, sympathy, and faith, immediately going to her Father God for assistance.

The Word shows us many varieties of prophets: writing prophets, weeping prophets, confronting prophets, end-time prophets, and building prophets. Isaiah, Ezekiel, and Amos were called "seeing prophets" as exemplified in the following passage of Scripture:

The vision of Isaiah the son of Amoz, which he saw concerning Judah and Jerusalem in the days of Uzziah, Jotham, Ahaz, and Hezekiah, kings of Judah. (Isaiah 1:1)

Now it came to pass in the thirtieth year, in the fourth month, on the fifth day of the month, as I was among the captives by the River Chebar, that the heavens were opened and I saw visions of God. (Ezekiel 1:1)

The words of Amos, who was among the sheep breeders of Tekoa, which he saw concerning Israel in the days of Uzziah king of Judah and in the days of Jeroboam the son of Joash, king of Israel, two years before the earthquake. (Amos 1:1)

Jeremiah and Hosea were known as "hearing prophets" as we note in these two references:

Then the word of the LORD came to me, saying .... (Jeremiah 1:4)

The word of the LORD that came to Hosea the son of Beeri, in the days of Uzziah, Jotham, Ahaz, and

Hezekiah, kings of Judah, and in the days of Jeroboam the son of Joash, king of Israel. (Hosea 1:1)

Because Mothers of Nations need to be prophetically developed, they will walk through an intense school of the Spirit. Their nature will need to be bold, confident, and able to function alone. The early years of their spiritual walk may have been trimmed to only the basics of life. Like John the Baptist, they may have found themselves surviving on honey and locusts—just the necessities. This personal sacrifice may not persist their entire lives. However long this period of testing lasts, it prepares them for their future assignments in ministry. Their belief system is traditional and focused. God's way may not always be the most comfortable way, but God's way is the only way!

These Mothers of Nations, like the prophets of old, are often passionate, intense, devoted, zealous, seasoned, enthusiastic, and emotional. Their feelings run deep. Like the watchman Jeremiah, they cry. Jeremiah was called a "weeping prophet." He felt pain over Israel's stubborn and rebellious nature which was God's pain expressed through him. He knew the devastation that awaited them, but he could not convince them to repent. No wonder he lamented, *"Is it nothing to you, all you who pass by? Behold and see if there is any sorrow like my sorrow ... "* (Lamentations 1:12). Like Jeremiah, Mothers of Nations feel the pain and carry a burden for the stubborn and rebellious, crying out to God for their deliverance.

Prophetically inclined Mothers of Nations are recognized as leaders with a Word from God. They have keys to unlock the Word or unlock a closed and hard heart. They have power to bind and loose. They can discern evil at work and address it with a level of such power and authority that it is brought to a standstill. These women have a deep-rooted understanding of how God works and operates.

I recall a burden I received from the LORD to pray back in 1986 concerning a young girl who was suddenly experiencing paralysis. The doctors thought she might have French polio. I went into my prayer closet and prayed for that young girl for hours. The prayer was extremely intense. I felt like I was wrestling with a demon. I kept hearing the words, "Don't let go until you get your blessing," so I kept praying until hours later when the burden lifted. When I finished I noticed that I had broken blood vessels in my hands, my face and my arms. The prayer was so strong that literally I had physical bruising! The next day I heard that the young girl was completely well and walking again. I know from personal experience that prayer and the prophetic word broke the power of that curse.

My favorite part of this prophetic aspect is watching the ministry of Mothers of Nations unfold as they learn to obey the LORD. These powerful women are able to bring life, love, and laughter through the power, passion, and presence of Christ. Every nation they go to has been changed by their presence. Every heart they minister to has felt their impact. Transformed from spiritual barrenness to life herself, the Mother of Nations knows how to be used by God to declare His glory among the nations, turning barren lands into fruitful fields that produce an eternal harvest for the King.

CHAPTER 15

MOTHERS OF NATIONS
ARE APOSTOLICALLY INCLINED

*"Truly the signs of an apostle were accomplished
among you with all perseverance,
in signs and wonders and mighty deeds."*
(2 Corinthians 12:12)

Mothers of Nations are found praying like the apostles of the early Church. They pray for a revelation of God's will for individuals and nations. They pray for increased fruitfulness, increased patience, and increased understanding. Their heart continually desires God's Kingdom work to be completed.

Mothers of Nations who are apostolic, prophetic prayer warriors:

- Pray that whatever is preached from the LORD will be established.

- Pray for grace, mercy, and compassion on all.

- Pray with authority, binding regional demonic spirits and loosing captives.

- Pray and tear down strongholds that try to hinder God's work.

- Pray for angels to be released in the area to assist in the work of ministry.

- Pray for insight and revelation in the Word and in the Spirit realm.

- Pray for God's will to be done.

- Pray that God will reveal His strategy for an area.

As servants, Mothers of Nations are like Paul, knowing they have no reason to boast. All the glory belongs to God. Their motivation is not to rule, but to serve and to co-operate with the people to whom God sends them. Biblically, apostles and prophets had a particular area or people group to whom they were assigned. Paul was called to the Gentile world. Peter was called to the Jewish people. St. Thomas was called to Asia in general and India in particular. Some were forbidden to go to certain areas. Paul was kept from Asia by the Holy Spirit and through a dream was sent to Macedonia (Acts 16:6-10). These apostles (a word meaning "sent ones") had people and areas assigned to them. They were sent with a message from God and a purpose to fulfill. Generals of power and prayer, they knew their authority in the spiritual realm.

Mothers of Nations are similar. Apostles often start and establish new works, ministries, or churches. They know where to go, what to do, and how to do it. Able to mobilize people and knowing the timing of the LORD for a project, they often take teams with them to start a new work. God sends them administrators, intercessors, teachers, evangelists, and others who come alongside to complete the apostolic assignments.

When the Holy Spirit started teaching me about the apostle, there were few books available on this subject. Each time I found a book on this topic I would devour it, trying to understand my feelings and my call. Just the thought of calling oneself an "apostle" was very frightening to me. I felt so undeserving. I thought, "After all, I am a female and have done so little compared to others."

But the truth was that I had initiated many ministry

works and I was continually helping others set their houses in order. One day I had a conversation with the LORD and mentioned to Him that apostles often are killed, hung, lose their heads, and the like. I told him that I wasn't sure I wanted a "title" that went along with these activities.

That evening I attended a ministry conference for pastors and a man that I highly respected called me to the altar. He began to rebuke me for wrestling with God on the very issue of accepting apostleship! I realized at that moment, female or male, no one has the right to tell God He doesn't know what He is doing. The term was settled in my heart that night and I accepted my position in Christ. You may be a Mother of Nations like me that just needs a prophet to say to you, "Stop wrestling with God's call on your life!"

Mothers of Nations ministering apostolically will plant churches, ordain elders, bring reforms, teach sound doctrine, raise up teams and team leaders, oversee ministries, bring correction, and even issue judgment if necessary. They will lay foundations and uproot others needing change. Often they will impart giftings, pray for a release of the Holy Spirit, and bring strategies to leaders by equipping, edifying, and encouraging the saints. Operating in signs, wonders, and miracles, they will expand the vision of everyone they meet and attract crowds. Some may criticize, complain, and even try to destroy them, but they just keep doing what God has put in their hearts to accomplish.

Mothers of Nations never see themselves as controlling others, for they respect the authority of God. Jesus did not like everything He saw or encountered, but He did not try to change it all at once or to control everyone to get it done. The apostles were able to operate in a corporate relationship to fulfill the Great Commission. A Mother of Nations has learned to cooperate in the Body of Christ and to come alongside other leadership with the heart of a God-sent helper.

Committed to Christ, she keeps herself humble, builds up her faith and confidence through the Word, and stays determined to complete her task on earth. Though she has risen to a pinnacle of purpose as an envoy of heaven, a history-maker and a world-changer, still to the very end she will be ever ruled by one simple thing - the devoted and loving heart of a Mother.

CHAPTER 16

MOTHERS OF NATIONS
ARE ANOINTED

"Plan and plant your gifts. Pray and play your role.
The harvest is assured when God manifests His
anointing power in your passionate actions."
Israelmore Ayivor,
Christian author and blogger from Ghana, Africa

As we come to the conclusion of this book, I realize there are so many other chapters that could be written about the qualities of a Mother of Nations, such as her fruitfulness, character, favor, and guidance. However, there is one final topic that I must address and that is the particular anointing that rests on a Mother of Nations. She can do nothing without the unction of the Holy Spirit operating in her life. The anointing will carry her through, help her flow in the gifts God has given her, and empower her to do the work of the ministry.

When Jesus started out in His ministry, He stood in the synagogue and proclaimed Isaiah 61:1-3 over Himself. This was a word that had been prophesied about the coming of an "Anointed One" who would change the world. This original passage reads as follows:

> *The Spirit of the LORD God is upon Me, because the LORD has anointed Me to preach good tidings to the poor; He has sent Me to heal the brokenhearted, to proclaim liberty to the captives, and the opening of the prison to those who are bound;*
> *To proclaim the acceptable year of the LORD, and the day of vengeance of our God; to comfort all who mourn,*
> *To console those who mourn in Zion, to give them beauty for ashes, the oil of joy for mourning, the garment*

of praise for the spirit of heaviness, that they may be called trees of righteousness, the planting of the LORD, that He may be glorified.

Luke 4:18-19 quotes Jesus as saying:

The Spirit of the LORD is upon Me, because He has anointed Me to preach the gospel to the poor; He sent Me to heal the brokenhearted, to proclaim liberty to the captives and recovery of sight to the blind, to set at liberty those who are oppressed;
To proclaim the acceptable year of the LORD.

When I first started out in ministry, I had no idea what to do. There was no one around to explain to me what I was experiencing, seeing, or hearing. A few ladies from Women's Aglow understood some things about ministry, but my experiences seemed to be different than theirs. Concerned that I might be getting off track or misled, I prayed and asked the LORD to help me understand my urges to pray, to prophesy, and to speak so boldly about the LORD.

The Holy Spirit guided me to 1 John 2:20, 27:

But you have an anointing from the Holy One, and you know all things …
But the anointing which you have received from Him abides in you, and you do not need that anyone teach you; but as the same anointing teaches you concerning all things, and is true, and is not a lie, and just as it has taught you, you will abide in Him.

These verses brought me such comfort as I realized I was in the school of the Holy Spirit! Man wouldn't be teaching me, rather God would. Years later the LORD brought men and women into my life and Bible school training to help me further in my spiritual development. I believe God has many

Mothers of Nations in locations where access to training isn't available, but the Holy Spirit is certainly available to them. It is the anointing that begins to guide, teach, and reveal the things we need to do and know.

One of my first experiences with the anointing on the mission field happened in India. I had gone there with my husband and a missionary friend who had started Peniel Bible College in Cochin, India. The missionary took my husband and me out to a remote area by bus. We stopped in the center of a little town and he handed me a portable microphone and said, "Preach!" Well, at that time in my life I had never preached or given an altar call for salvation. Yet the LORD had told me earlier that I was anointed to preach so I just opened my mouth and spoke. I do not remember what I said, but I spoke as the Holy Spirit told me what to say over the microphone. An Indian interpreted, and toward the end he took my message and turned it to a time of prayer for salvation. I have no idea how many were touched but many in the city streets heard what we had to say.

Later that same day my Indian friend took us out on the street to witness and he said to me, "Draw a crowd." Looking at him like he was crazy, my mind went absolutely blank. I couldn't remember even one Scripture verse, but I did think of the story of Paul falling off his horse on the road to Damascus. So I began to tell that account to the people walking by us. I remember saying that there was this man who was on his way to kill some Christians and God knocked him right off his horse. My mind was telling me that I must be crazy, but my spirit was telling me to keep talking. And as I kept speaking, people continued to stop and listen until a crowd gathered, and souls came into the Kingdom that day, all because of the anointing of God on this willing vessel.

The anointing in our lives can be extremely powerful as God uses us to lift off burdens or break bondages in other people. One time in India my friend and I were introduced to a new pastor's wife who was suffering from seizures. She seldom left her home or went out in public due to her condition. We learned that two other women previous to us had shared God's power to heal with her and sown spiritual seeds in her life before we ministered to her. As we talked the anointing came on us to share God's plan for her life and His healing power to set captives free. Through anointed prayer and counsel, we broke the power of fear over her life, giving her revelation and hope for her future potential. The anointing unveiled a whole new view of God's love for her and for others. Indeed, another Mother of Nations came alive that day.

Currently, this woman and her husband oversee three orphanages, a public K-12 school of 400 children, many church congregations, a movie production company, sewing schools, agricultural projects, and they are now building a hospital. This lady is also producing her own Gospel television show! Most certainly, the anointing broke the yoke over her life and has produced much fruit. As Isaiah 10:27 declares:

> It shall come to pass in that day that his burden will be taken away from your shoulder, and his yoke from your neck, and the yoke will be destroyed because of the anointing oil.

Truly, her yoke of fear was destroyed because of the anointing.

In the Philippines, Viet Nam, Cambodia, Thailand, Uganda, Kenya and other countries we have taught on the anointing and have encountered numerous supernatural experiences over the years. Once in the Philippines we were asked to help with the planting of a new church in Lucena City. The church was meeting in a local disco bar as they started out with the new congregation. One particular evening I was speaking on the topic of angels and the power of the anointing brought an angelic demonstration into the room. All of a sudden flashing balls of light appeared, racing from one side of the room to the other. At first we were wondering what was going on, but suddenly, people were falling over under the presence of the Spirit, experiencing visions and trances. One man saw his whole ministry in vision form. Another saw ministry ideas for the future. Several people felt totally renewed and everyone knew they had experienced a heavenly encounter.

The following week as I was pondering that occurrence, I received a newsletter from Charles and Francis Hunter. In that document they shared their recent experience of "flashing balls of light" in one of their ministry meetings. They called it "an angelic visitation." I knew exactly what they were talking about, as we had been in a very similar supernatural encounter.

I have had experiences with angels on different occasions as well. Once while driving, I felt the hands of an angel move my car to the side of the road and then I heard a voice say, "Stop the car." I did exactly that as I yielded to the hands directing my vehicle. Later we discovered there was a collision up the road in which we would have been hit head-on had we not been detained. My angel kept me from an accident.

Years ago, while living in St. Cloud, Minnesota, the head intercessor for Women's Aglow came to my house with her husband and told me that we needed to pray together immediately. She said God had spoken to her while shopping at the mall that she should get to my house and pray. We went downstairs to the family room with my children and began to intercede. As we prayed, we heard a storm outside. It sounded severe, but really we paid little attention to it. While praying I saw two angels standing on an inclined lawn lifting something up over their heads. These angels were taller than my house and so big that I could not see their heads as they disappeared into the sky.

After we finished praying and decided to go upstairs for coffee, the phone rang. It was my husband calling, wanting to make sure I was safe. He had heard on the radio that a tornado had passed through our neighborhood a few minutes earlier. I told him it had stormed but I did not know about the tornado. All of a sudden helicopters were overhead, and police cars were coming into our housing development. Then I realized something serious had just happened.

Later that night we found out that a tornado had come through the area right toward my house. But something happened to lift it up off my lawn and it went back down behind our home. Debris was everywhere except in my yard. God had spared my home and life due to the obedience of an anointed prayer warrior learning the call to pray.

Angels come when we ask! In my case, they saved my life, my children, and my neighbors' lives. Some of our neighbors lost their homes, but all of them had miracle stories as to how their lives were spared. Certainly angels were on assignment that day and we were so glad that we had yielded to the anointing to pray!

In 2001 I wrote and published a book titled *The Lion Anointing*. During my research I came across this verse in Proverbs 28:1, *"The wicked flee when no one pursues, but the righteous are bold as a lion."* As God's children, He has made us the kings and queens of this jungle called earth. Adam and Eve were put here to rule and reign over all. Unfortunately, they sinned and their dominion was lost temporarily.

But God said that He would send a child through the tribe of Judah, which is the "lion" tribe. Hebrews 7:14 tells us, *"For it is evident that our LORD arose from Judah, of which tribe Moses spoke nothing concerning priesthood."* Jesus is an offspring of the tribe of Judah, sent by God to change things.

As I was meditating on various scriptures mentioning lions one day, I happened to look up at a painting on my wall of a lion and lamb lying down together. The Holy Spirit began to speak to my spirit and say, "I have anointed you to operate as a lamb, but now I will teach you to also be like a lion." Mothers of Nations have both natures – lamb and lion—and need to be able to move from one nature to the other, depending upon their circumstances.

Under the anointing of the LORD we can see the devil for who he is. We also learn to feed on the Word, just as a lion or lamb need water and food. To me, the apostolic nature is a lion in spirit. Lions know their territory, are willing to fight until the battle is won, and they are bold and aggressive when necessary.

As a Mother of Nations God will anoint you for what He needs you to do. A friend of mine went to Africa with me and visited a Christian school. While walking on the school grounds she felt the LORD speak to her to build a science building there in her mother's name. Her mother had been a teacher and she wanted to honor her.

Anointed and appointed for an assignment from God, my friend went back to the United States and called all her siblings, nieces, nephews, and others related to her mother and told them about the building project idea in Africa. In just a few months she and her relatives had raised enough money to build the science wing. Her elderly mother was so blessed to know that her daughter had helped to build part of a school for children in another country and very honored that they named the building after her. It's her heritage for many years to come as a Mother of Nations.

Many times when I have taken women on mission trips to other countries they have received anointed ideas and returned home to accomplish them. One lady raised support for students in a school for the blind where girls learned furniture making by weaving. Interesting, the lady who runs the school is also blind. Another minister friend is helping orphanages financially. Other Mothers of Nations are putting individual children through school because their parents are too poor to do so.

In Uganda we have built playgrounds, basketball courts, and boxing gyms. Women have assisted in getting a young man a prosthetic eye. Other Mothers of Nations have purchased bicycles for pastors, supported medical outreach camps, and carried out many other creative ideas—all because the anointing of God was at work in their lives to make a difference in the lives of others.

I have learned that the anointing varies in depth, as well as in length. Sometimes it is so deep you cannot move. Once I was preaching in Canada and no one could get near me at the altar time without being knocked back because the anointing was so thick. Ushers had to hold me up and escort people to me so I could pray for them.

The previous night's meeting had been difficult as, unknown to me, the church that had invited me was in the middle of a split. One lady responsible for organizing the conference had stayed up all night praying, requesting God to pour out His Spirit in power. He heard her prayers and the anointing on that next night's meeting was more powerful than anything I had ever seen. Women had visions, words of knowledge, and saw their own sins. The last day we were united in spirit and truth due to the power and work of the anointing.

Psalm 89:19-29 lists many characteristics and manifestations that result from the anointing being in a person's life. Let's read through that passage first.

Then You spoke in a vision to Your holy one, and said: "I have given help to one who is mighty; I have exalted one chosen from the people.

I have found My servant David; with My holy oil I have anointed him,

With whom My hand shall be established; also My arm shall strengthen him.

The enemy shall not outwit him, nor the son of wickedness afflict him.

I will beat down his foes before his face, and plague those who hate him.

But My faithfulness and My mercy shall be with him, and in My name his horn shall be exalted.

Also I will set his hand over the sea, and his right hand over the rivers."

He shall cry to Me, "You are my Father, My God, and the rock of my salvation."

Also I will make him My firstborn, the highest of the kings of the earth.

My mercy I will keep for him forever, and My covenant shall stand firm with him.

His seed also I will make to endure forever, and his throne as the days of heaven.

In these verses we see that the anointing brings:

- God's help
- Exaltation and authority
- God's hand on us
- God's strength
- Freedom from deception and the wicked
- Victory over enemies
- God's faithfulness and lovingkindness
- Influence over the nations
- Father / son relationship
- Membership in the church of first-born
- Participation in God's covenant
- Establishment of descendants forever

When is the anointing evident? I have discovered that the anointing is evident when:

1. God goes beyond our natural abilities, imparting supernatural ability.

2. A speaker flows into an unexpected vein of ministry.

3. The conscious sense of God's abiding and moving Presence appears.

4. A leader's message brings spiritual results in the lives of his/her hearers.

5. Repentance comes.

6. Healings occur.

7. People are encouraged and edified by worship.

8. A broken heart is healed.

9. Jesus is glorified and the Kingdom of God advances.

Last of all, we see that the anointing is needed to produce fruit. God uses the anointing on our lives to change the world and us. In Hebrew, the words for anointing mean "to overflow, to satisfy, to produce light, to rub with oil, to consecrate, to smear over with oil, or to make rich or fat."

When God gave us the Holy Spirit, along with the Spirit came the anointing (the specific application of His Spirit to fulfill a certain purpose or purposes). We need to be open to flowing in the Spirit and allowing God to use us to minister in the anointing. Sometimes it might be for consecration, a time of being separated unto God. Other times the anointing may be a vehicle to bring light or revelation to our circumstance.

In 1 Samuel 16:1-13, David was anointed King. The horn filled with oil represented an infilling of God's character, God's nature and supernatural empowerment. Samuel was asked to use the horn of oil when anointing David. The LORD had David anointed by Samuel in this way to release purpose, to develop character in his life, to set him apart, and to commission him into a position of authority.

David made mistakes along the way, but the one thing he never wanted to lose was the Holy Spirit, or what we also call the anointing. David kept his heart pure before God, as he knew the anointing on his life depended upon it. Even after sinning with Bathsheba, David cried out to God that God would not take His Spirit from him. He never wanted to lose God's anointing on his life or ministry.

There is no other thing given to us as Mothers of Nations that is more precious than God's anointing. Jesus gave His life that we could receive Him and His anointing. Let's treasure Him and the price He paid that we might walk in His Spirit and carry His anointing!

Truly, Mothers of Nations change their world because of this anointing. May the anointing of God's Holy Spirit fill you. May His anointing grace you for all the circumstances and situations you face in your life. And may His anointing empower you to be an unstoppable Mother of Nations!

EPILOGUE

ARE YOU A MOTHER OF NATIONS?

A re you a Mother of Nations? Have you found that you truly identify with these characteristics of a Mother of Nations? If so, we would like to hear from you!

Tell us about yourself and the work you are doing in the Kingdom of God. We would like to pray for you regularly and encourage you in your ministry. We know that ministry can be a lonely place and sometimes one phone call, one prophecy, one prayer, or one message can keep a person going for a long time. Please contact us at:

Women's International Minister's Network (WIMN)
c/o Resurrection Life Church and World Ministry Center
ATTN: Dr. Sharon Predovich
16397 Glory Lane
Eden Prairie, MN 55344 U.S.A.
You may also email us at:
mothersofnations@aol.com

Now let us pray for you.

Dear heavenly Father,

We thank you for this Mother of Nations. She has been fashioned and framed by You and is in the process of being fully developed. You have a destiny especially designed for her to fulfill and a people group for her to influence. May You sovereignly touch her right now with Your love and warmth. May Your words become revelations of life and power to her. May she be strengthened, encouraged, and kept safe all the days of her life and may she dwell in Your presence forever. Amen.

We love you, Mother of Nations! Keep up the good work and be abundantly blessed and fruitful. For the LORD appointed you that you should *"go and bear fruit, and that your fruit should remain"* (John 15:16).

Dr. Sharon Predovich
A Mother of Nations

POEM

MOTHER OF NATIONS

Dedicated to my mother Apostle Sharon Predovich
by Aimee Kyambadde (1999)

Lovingkindness, always willing to serve another.

Giving spirit, helping others to fulfill their dreams.

Beautiful presence, radiating the glory of God.

Humble heart, forgiving the foolish and
*   unknown things.*

Spirit of restoration, replenishing people
*   through relationship.*

Gracious soul, thoughtful in good and bad times.

Patient woman, full of mercy.

Tender strength, reaching to the lost and lonely.

Faithful encourager, crying out for the hurting.

Bold adventurer, willing to obey God at any cost.

Teacher, friend and mentor.

You are a Mother to the Nations.

I am one of your legacies—
*   another Mother of Nations.*

My Daughter, Aimee Kyambadde
Missionary to Uganda and a Mother of Nations

Aimee and her husband David.

I thank the LORD that my daughter Aimee Kyambadde (www.redeemedafrica.com) has received the same mantle to become a Mother of Nations. She is serving the LORD in Uganda, Africa, as a pastor, pastor's wife, mother of two children, mother to over forty street children, preacher, teacher, developer of youth programs, and outreaches to musicians, athletes and much more. The poem she wrote for me on the previous page is a special ministry treasure of mine. I pray it blesses you as well.

PHOTO GALLERY

Asian Mother receives the call to yet another nation.

*Transportation
to minister
sometimes
means by foot!*

Burdens for nations came at this border prayer time.

Mothers rejoice in blessing other ministry leadership.

Preaching in the heat of the day to Philippine leadership.

Intercessory prayer mission to China.

Indian leadership … so hungry for the Word of God!

Young lady's swollen legs and feet healed at a prayer meeting.

Indian woman seeking the Lord at a house meeting.

School and orphanage staff in central India.

Presenting Indian Pastors with new Bibles.

Indian Women's Conference attendees.

Visit to Mt. Olive Prayer Center prayer cells in Kenya.

Ministering to Kenyan Mother in Nairobi.

Ministering with Birmingham, England women's leadership.

Late night BBC radio interview in Birmingham, England.

Mother to Uganda, Dr. Sharon's daughter Aimee Predovich Kyambadde.

Young men of Home Again, ministry of Dr. Sharon's daughter and son-in-law in Kampala, Uganda.

Blankets purchased for Ugandan prison ministry.

Ugandan pastors receive new bicycles for ministry transportation.

Dr. Sharon and her friend General Charles Angina, Deputy Army Commander Uganda Peoples Defense Forces.

Dr. Sharon and the Ugandan boy of her spiritual dream.